WALK
IN
FAITH

WALK IN FAITH

5-Minute Devotions for Teen Guys

Andy Dooley

Illustrations by Andrzej Wieteszka

ALTHEA
PRESS

Interior and Cover Designer: Suzanne LaGasa
Photo Art Director: Sue Bischofberger
Editor: Bridget Fitzgerald
Production Editor: Andrew Yackira
Illustrations: Andrzej Wieteszka

ISBN: Print 978-1-64152-282-3 | eBook 978-1-64152-283-0

To my best friend, my wife Tiffany. And to my son Andy II for being an inspiration to me. I look forward to reading this with you.

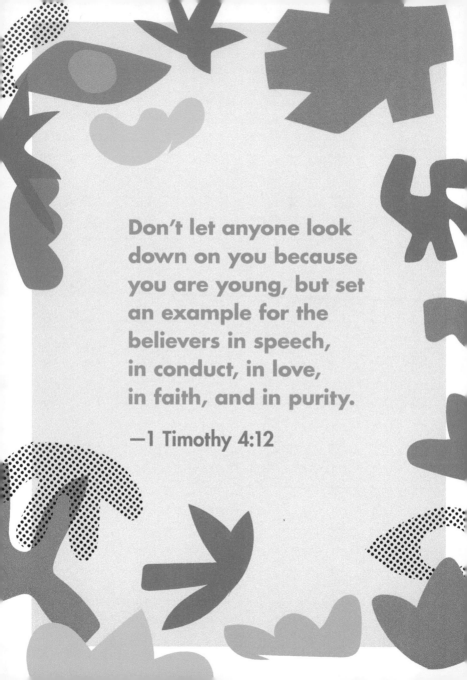

Don't let anyone look down on you because you are young, but set an example for the believers in speech, in conduct, in love, in faith, and in purity.

—1 Timothy 4:12

INTRODUCTION

Teen guys have it easy—but you also have it rough. You have it all figured out and nothing figured out at all. You love life, but sometimes you can't stand life. The reality of a teenager is full of contradictions. But that's part of what makes this phase of life so exciting. You know what else is exciting? The fact that teen guys—all of you—are the next generation of strong male leaders.

As a young teen, I sought guidance: I wanted to feel loved and happy—even if that didn't always show on the surface. Then, throughout high school, I realized that I felt most fulfilled when I had the honor of offering guidance to my peers, and so I participated in a mentorship program as a senior. Once in college, I made an effort to get to know the kids in the local community. Why? Because I knew what it was like to be a young man in the world. It's not easy to navigate the choppy waters of young adulthood; some of us need all the help we can get.

One of the hardest aspects of this time of your life is knowing whom you can talk to—and, even more than that, knowing whom you can trust and open up to. I was fortunate to grow up with great parents who loved, supported, inspired, and motivated me to be a man of God. Still, that didn't keep me from experiencing the confusion, rejections, temptations, triumphs, and all the other ups and downs of being a teenager. I created this devotional as a way to help you along your journey. My hope is that it becomes a trusted source of comfort and guidance—that it encourages you to live your best life, in a way that makes life better for others.

Remember: You are not too young to raise the bar in society. You are not too young to be a beacon of light for your family, peers, and community. If you can grasp the true facts about how God sees you and his desires for you to live a blessed life, you will be nothing less than a world changer.

Anger, romantic feelings, siblings, depression, addiction, jealousy, stress, and creativity—these are just a few of the topics I address in this book, along with other nagging questions about life today. Each devotion starts with a piece of Scripture relating to the topic at hand, followed by a relatable story or life lesson, and then a short question or reflection. You can work through the book from start to finish or skip around to the topics that feel most relevant to you on any given day.

My prayer is that this devotional will become a book that you want with you at all times. When you leave your house, you'll make sure you have your cell phone, your Bible, and this devotional—if not in hand then in mind. Let it serve as your cheat sheet for a successful, fulfilling, godly lifestyle.

WHY ARE THEY DOING THIS?

Do not take revenge, my dear friends, but leave room for God's wrath, for it is written: "It is mine to avenge; I will repay," says the LORD.

—Romans 12:19

Recently a middle school kid asked me at youth group, "Why are they doing this?" He was referring to school shootings. I took a moment to really think about his question, and then he said, "I want revenge." I had compassion for his hurt and anger. But I told him that as hard as it was to understand, it wasn't his battle to avenge. The fight belongs to the Lord.

I know that some of you deal with violence regularly. Maybe your neighborhood isn't safe, or there are fights every day at your school. This type of violence—and the violence in the news every day—affects you deeply. But trust me when I tell you that you don't have to fight these battles. Leave the hard part to God. He said, "Leave room for God's wrath." He wants you to sit back and let him step up on your behalf.

Remember that acts of violence are coming from broken individuals who operate out of selfishness, anger, and pride. Only Jesus can change their hearts. Not you. The way you can help is by living out your faith via positive actions and prayers. Instead of following others who you know are doing wrong, raise the bar and lead them another way.

REFLECT:

What battles are you facing right now that God could step in and fight for you? If you feel hungry for revenge, can you turn it over to God and act another way instead?

DO WORK!

Whatever you do, work at it with all your heart, as working for the Lord,
not for human masters.

—Colossians 3:23

Work might feel like a four-letter word sometimes. But it's far from a bad word—it's the catalyst for change, for achieving your dreams, and for connecting to your purpose. In those times when you don't feel like working hard for your teachers, coaches, bosses, or parents, know that you don't actually work for them. Try to replace their faces with the image of God, the Creator of this universe and the author of your life story.

A guy name Paul in the Bible realized that he was called to ministry and to share the Gospel with everyone unapologetically. He worked hard to carry out the plan for his life, and he was brutally beaten and ridiculed. Most people would quit in the face of so much adversity, but he knew that he was working unto the Lord, so he would get back up and return to his life mission with a passion only God can motivate.

God wants to use you in so many areas of life. Why limit yourself by not working hard and not giving it your all? With God, you kick down limitations and open the door to unlimited possibilities. You have desires and dreams downloaded in your heart. Remember that your boss is the Lord, and it is time to do work!

REFLECT:

What responsibilities (paid or not) have you felt unmotivated about lately? What are two action steps you can take this week to stay motivated in your duties and bring your best to the work ahead?

YOU WERE CREATED TO MAKE AN IMPACT

Get wisdom, get understanding; do not forget my words or turn away from them. Do not forsake wisdom, and she will protect you; love her, and she will watch over you.

—Proverbs 4:5–6

We all have the desire to make an impact with our lives, through our relationships, wealth, sports, music, teaching, acting, or another calling. Most of the time, the impact we want to make is for our own personal fulfillment. True fulfillment, however, is found only by using our gifts and talents to make an impact for God, which requires us to ask for and apply wisdom in our lives.

There are two different types of impact we can have: earthly and eternal. An earthly impact is driven by self, fame, or the desire to impress others. An eternal impact results from fulfilling the plan that God has for our lives.

Just as God used wisdom to create the universe (Proverbs 8:22–36), we also need to use wisdom to create a life that makes an eternal impact. In Proverbs 4:5, Solomon states, "Get wisdom! Get understanding!"

We must apply God's wisdom to our everyday lives—otherwise we will fall victim to our own self-destruction. We each have our own will, and many times it is contrary to the will of God. The good news is that in Christ we are made righteous, and through the Holy Spirit we can yield our will to God's.

REFLECT:

How can you make an eternal impact right now?
Here are a few ideas:
- *Have a good attitude toward your parents.*
- *Make new friends.*
- *Pay for someone's lunch.*
- *Start a Bible club at your school.*

> One who has unreliable friends soon comes to ruin,
> but there is a friend who sticks closer than a brother.
>
> —Proverbs 18:24

One thing I know is that we are imperfect people. You will have different types of friends along your journey. Some will come and go, and others will stay in your life—for a season or a lifetime. Regardless of who it is, you will never have a friend like Jesus. Hebrews 13:8 says, "Jesus Christ is the same yesterday and today and forever." That means he has never changed, and never will.

I thought my boy in high school was a constant. I knew he wasn't Jesus, but I also knew I could count on him. We practiced sports, we played video games, we shared goals and dreams—and we talked about girls. Unfortunately, he went behind my back and spilled some secrets, and I was so hurt that I thought I would never trust another friend again.

Many of us have the desire to have a lot of friends. While that's not necessarily a bad desire, Scripture warns us that having a lot of unreliable friends can stretch us too thin and lead us to destruction. Jesus is the one friend you can trust completely. He accepts the real you. He loves the imperfect you. He will love you no matter what you are going through.

REFLECT:
Who are the friends you can truly rely on? Do you need to let go of any friendships?

TURN THE LIGHT ON

He said to them, "Do you bring in a lamp to put it under a bowl or a bed? Instead,
don't you put it on its stand? For whatever is hidden is meant to be disclosed,
and whatever is concealed is meant to be brought out into the open."

—Mark 4:21–22

Sometimes the fear of getting in trouble or being judged will compel you to hide information you should share. It's not easy to shed light on a tough situation; it's often easier to cover it up. But when we keep things secret, it can darken our life experience.

One guy I had the privilege of mentoring had a lot of secrets. They were weighing him down spiritually and emotionally. He went from being the life of the party to rarely smiling and crying often. The secrets ate him up and made him feel ashamed, scared, unworthy, and depressed. We sat down and had a heart-to-heart about how he could begin to free himself of this burden.

I had Mark 4:21–22 in mind when I told him the importance of bringing his secrets out into the open. I said, "I'm here for you, and I'll go through this process with you. And when you go home, remember that your parents love you, God loves you, and you will find freedom by telling them what is going on."

That hard conversation with his parents was the beginning of his new life. He turned the light on his secrets and chased darkness away.

REFLECT:
What secrets do you have? Turn the light on. Figure out the best person in your life to share them with, and open up honestly. Remember that God knows all your secrets. Think of this first the next time you consider doing something you may want to hide.

IT WASN'T ME!

The LORD detests lying lips, but he delights in people who are trustworthy.
—Proverbs 12:22

Once, when I was about 12 years old, a creepy cat followed me home. I didn't like how the cat was staring me down (I'd had a bad experience with a cat as a little kid, and I remembered it well), so I had to do something.

I bent down and picked up a rock—only the size of a quarter—and, without hesitation, threw it in the cat's direction. The cat, of course, easily evaded the rock, and it shattered a window instead. I stood there in shock as my neighbor opened the door and saw me looking in her direction. "What happened to my window?" she yelled. I immediately pointed in the opposite direction and lied, "Those guys threw a rock through your window and ran away."

She went looking for them, and I ran two doors down to my house. Minutes later the doorbell rang, and my dad answered. It wasn't long before I was called down, and I knew I was caught. I confessed, tears streaming down my face. And although I was in trouble, I immediately felt lighter.

Satan has a nickname: the father of lies. Ouch! He delights in those who cannot be trusted. Don't be one of them. Own up. Lying only separates you from God.

REFLECT:
Is there anything you've lied about recently?
If so, ask God for forgiveness and repent. Start fresh with a clean slate and make a commitment to abstain from lying.

WHAT AM I GOOD AT?

Each of you should use whatever gift you have received to serve others, as faithful stewards of God's grace in its various forms. If anyone speaks, they should do so as one who speaks the very words of God. If anyone serves, they should do so with the strength God provides, so that in all things God may be praised through Jesus Christ. To him be the glory and the power for ever and ever. Amen.

—1 Peter 4:10–11

You have special gifts and talents that are unique to you and to your life's purpose. In this stage of life, it's normal to not know exactly what gifts dwell inside of you. But it's never too early to start investigating those talents.

Are you a naturally great athlete?

Can you freestyle rap?

Can you draw really well?

When you speak, do people listen and follow what you say?

Is math easy for you?

Can you remember a lot of information that you read?

When you sing, do people want to hear you sing more?

These are just a few questions to start asking yourself to discover your unique calling.

First Peter 4:10–11 explains that your gifts are not just for you; they are meant to serve others—just as Jesus came to this world to serve you and give everyone a chance at eternal life. Never forget that the talent you possess is God's gift and should be used to point others to Jesus.

REFLECT:
Write down what you are good at, what you are passionate about, and what comes easiest to you. Then ask God to reveal to you your purpose here on earth.

YOUR WORDS CARRY WEIGHT

The tongue has the power of life and death, and those who love it will eat its fruit.
—Proverbs 18:21

Your words have immense power—they can tear down a person or lift their spirits. Likewise, what you say about yourself can positively or negatively impact your life. Your words are born from the womb of your heart. If your heart is good and full of positivity, your words will produce good fruit—that is, your words will take you on a path that you will benefit from.

We've all heard someone say, "That was random." Your words are never random. A person's speech is a mirror image of their moral compass. I want to encourage you to think before you speak. When you are around your friends, pay attention to how you talk and to the thoughts behind your words. Ask yourself, *Do I want these words to have the power of life or death?*

And think about the words you use when speaking about yourself. God created you; don't ever say negative things about yourself. Those words can penetrate like a bee sting. They have the ability to affect a small part of your life—or, like an allergy, they can cause the entire system to break down and drastically alter your future. If someone speaks ill of you, make sure you don't receive or internalize it. Immediately combat it with words of blessings to yourself and others.

REFLECT:
- *Your words have power. Think before you speak. Catch yourself before speaking ill of yourself of others.*
- *Memorize Psalm 139:13–15.*
- *Practice speaking life to people you talk to.*

THE KEY TO SUCCESS IS HUMILITY

Humble yourselves, therefore, under God's mighty hand, that he may lift you up in due time. Cast all your anxiety on him because he cares for you.

—1 Peter 5:6–7

If you want to be successful in life, let humility become one of your superpowers. Humility brings about order and peace while pride brings chaos and tension. There will be moments when your peers and life in general will test your desire to be humble. I urge you to choose humility over pride every time.

With success, it's easy to flirt with pride. 1 Peter 5:6–7 says to humble yourself to God's mighty hand. If you are able to stay humble, God can trust you with the success and gifts that you have. With that trust he will elevate you at the right time. Everything is beautiful in God's timing, so let him direct your life. And when you get anxious or impatient, talk with God, show him your concerns, and let him work out the details.

REFLECT:

Reflecting on how huge, marvelous, and powerful God is should bring humility into your heart.
Think about ways you can be more humble.
- *Listen more, talk less.*
- *Appreciate the talents of others.*
- *Be coachable.*
- *Never stop learning.*
- *Ask for feedback.*

I CHOOSE JOY

*"This day is holy to our L*ORD*. Do not grieve, for the joy of the L*ORD *is your strength."*
—Nehemiah 8:10

My dad served in the military and was a pastor, so his parenting style was both strict and loving. In seventh grade I realized how much I enjoyed playing sports. The only problem was that I started to put less effort into my homework. My dad noticed and told me that if I didn't finish my homework, I couldn't go to football practice. I never thought that he would follow through—I was the captain on my team, so he wouldn't truly make me miss practice. What kind of an example of a leader would that be?

Of course, he found out that I forgot to do a homework assignment and barred me from football. He upped the ante too by saying, "You will show up to practice and let the team know why you can't participate."

I was devastated and embarrassed that day, but my dad taught me well. I mustered up my courage, admitted my wrongdoing, and chose to wholeheartedly support my teammates from the sidelines.

You will have good and bad days, and it's how you respond that shapes your day—and your future. Choose joy. It's not easy when you have to lay down your pride. Choosing joy on a bad day helps us develop our inner strength so we can be used by God.

REFLECT:
Joy is a choice. You must make a choice between the reality of everyday life and God's supernatural joy.
What friendship, relationship, or pressure in your life right now might require you to choose joy?
Ask the Holy Spirit to bring you supernatural joy in those areas.

Don't let anyone look down on you because you are young, but set an example for the believers in speech, in conduct, in love, in faith and in purity.

—1 Timothy 4:12

I don't want anyone to grow up too fast, but as a Christian, you are set apart. You are not too young to be used by God to impact those around you—your friends, parents, siblings, or followers.

Oftentimes, young people are looked down upon because they are stereotyped as being immature, selfish, rude, entitled, rebellious, and a host of other annoying labels. These descriptions don't speak to you or your future, yet they can cause people to judge an entire generation.

It isn't fair, and that's why Paul told Timothy in the Bible, "Don't let anyone look down on you because of your youth." You can change the game and set an example for your peers and older generations by the way you talk and conduct yourself, your faith in God, and your pursuit of purity. Don't disrespect the generation before you; instead, honor and revere them. There is only one standard, and that is God's standard. Ask questions and be willing to learn—no one can despise you if you inspire them to be better.

Imagine being the catalyst for a generation of young people who are truly hungry to know God and be used by him. You literally can change the world!

REFLECT:

Ask God to reveal his standard of living every time you read your Bible. It's never too early to start. You will raise the standards of the people around you by your actions.

I'M UPSET!

A person's wisdom yields patience; it is to one's glory to overlook an offense.
—Proverbs 19:11

God recognizes that we will get angry. While sometimes it's okay to show that emotion, sin creeps in when we let it control us. You must exercise self-control and know how to take a step back before letting anger take over your character. Unfortunately, not everybody you encounter will be a Christian or know how to manage their anger.

You may be wondering how you do this.

> *How do I not allow anger to control me when I am made fun of at school every week?*
>
> *How do I not allow anger to control me when I'm the victim of racial slurs?*
>
> *How do I not allow anger to control me when I lose? I hate losing!*
>
> *How do I not allow anger to control me when my girlfriend cheats on me or breaks up with me?*

These are just a few things that you—and your peers—may be dealing with. In order to control your anger you must exercise patience and not rush to react. Find the calm within your storm and take a moment to evaluate the situation. Ask God for wisdom. Time, patience, and godly wisdom will guide you to work out your issue with a calmer demeanor.

REFLECT:

Whenever you have a situation that makes you upset and angry, do the following:
- *Pray for God to give you peace and wisdom in your situation.*
- *Pray for the person you're upset with.*
- *Ask God to change your heart.*

YOU WILL OVERCOME

"I have told you these things, so that in me you may have peace. In this world you will have trouble. But take heart! I have overcome the world."

—John 16:33

It was my first week of school: new middle school, new neighborhood, new everything. I was an excited army kid who enjoyed moving around and meeting new people. One day in homeroom we had some free time. I was sketching and asked the kid across from me if I could borrow his black marker. He looked at me and said, "Why don't you just use your finger? You're black." Without thinking, I jumped out of my seat and punched him in the face. Right away the teacher separated us, and we were sent to the office. I thought to myself, *My parents are going to be so mad when I get suspended in my first week of school.*

I admitted to the principal that my actions weren't right, regardless of how wrong the comment was. The other boy was suspended, and I received a warning. But his remark taught me to dread meeting new people, and I was in a state of sadness for a long while.

In order to find peace and overcome the world's obstacles, we must realize troubles will come in and out of our lives. Jesus overcame brutal pain so that through him you could surmount any obstacle. I was stuck in my feelings until I opened up and welcomed them. It was only in sharing my experience that I learned I was not alone.

REFLECT:

If you are sad, please open up to someone you trust and share your feelings. Then go to God and ask him for peace that surpasses all understanding during this time of sadness.

BE THE BEST TEAMMATE EVER

Two are better than one, because they have a good return for their labor.
—Ecclesiastes 4:9

Whether you're working on a group project, acting in a play, practicing on a sports team, or playing in a band, you should always strive to be the best teammate ever.

You hold the power to add value to your team or group. Scripture states that two are better than one. You can accomplish more when you come together. Friendship is a team effort. When you get married someday in the future, that union will be your ultimate friendship, and together you'll be the ultimate team. Working with others teaches you how to share and receive information, work with different personalities toward a common goal, and collaborate effectively. Being a team player isn't easy. It takes hard work and humility. Through teamwork, ordinary guys can come together to do extraordinary things.

Let's be honest—Jesus probably didn't need a team. Yet he assembled 12 young guys to assist in the work of the kingdom. It took a group effort to have great success in ministry. Even though Jesus would have been considered the star player, he made a point to be the best teammate he could be.

REFLECT:
Think about all the teams you're on right now—including those related to sports, school projects, your friends, and your family. Commit to being the best teammate ever. This mind-set will help you succeed in life, and it will expand your influence.
Ask yourself, In what ways could I be a better teammate?
List them and try to apply them.

GET UP, GET OUT, AND GET SOME

As vinegar to the teeth and smoke to the eyes, so are sluggards to those who send them.
—Proverbs 10:26

Homework can be time-consuming and exhausting. At times it may feel pointless, but the deal is, you have to do it to get good grades. I know you probably think it would be nice if you could just sleep in, eat breakfast (that someone else has prepared), and lie around on the couch watching TV, scrolling through social media, or playing video games.

It sounds pretty cool until you realize how God feels about laziness. Proverbs 10:26 gives you a vivid description of a lazy person: They're like vinegar, pungent and displeasing in your mouth. Like smoke in your eyes, stinging and irritating.

God strongly dislikes laziness, and so should you. Thank goodness he wasn't lazy in creating this world, creating us, or giving us a chance at eternal life by sending his only Son to die on a cross for our sins. Approach life knowing that God expects more effort from you—more effort in the classroom, more effort with helping your parents around the house, more effort in taking care of your health, more effort in spending time with him, more effort in sharing the Gospel with others.

REFLECT:
Here are some practical ways to fight laziness:
  - *Write down a vision for your life. Whom do you want to be? What do you want to do?*
  - *Get off the couch. Get active by working out or playing a sport.*
  - *Set goals.*
  - *Take one day at a time.*
  - *Read more about how God feels about laziness in the book of Proverbs.*

PROTECT YOUR EYES

Dear children, do not let anyone lead you astray. The one who does what is right is righteous, just as he is righteous. The one who does what is sinful is of the devil, because the devil has been sinning from the beginning. The reason the Son of God appeared was to destroy the devil's work. No one who is born of God will continue to sin, because God's seed remains in them; they cannot go on sinning, because they have been born of God.

—1 John 3:7–9

It has become increasingly difficult to protect your eyes. You have so much thrown your way on a daily basis—whether in the locker room, on social media, elsewhere online, or on TV. I know pornography can be hard to avoid and a temptation. But "do not let anyone lead you astray."

Watching pornography is a sin because you are lusting after someone who is not your wife and therefore committing sexual sin against your body. God says to run from sexual immorality. In 1 John 3:7–9, the message is plain and simple. If you continue to sin knowingly, you are operating under the devil.

Satan wants you to fall victim to temptation—and then to sin. You need to be proactive. I won't lie to you, it will be a constant battle—but there are ways to protect your eyes.

REFLECT:

Here are practical ways to protect your eyes.
- *If you have a problem watching porn, you must admit that you have a problem.*
- *Talk to someone so you can start healing. Pray 1 John 3:7–9 to yourself daily. "Turn my eyes away from worthless things; preserve my life according to your word" (Psalm 119:37).*
- *Download an app called Covenant Eyes. It helps monitor what you look at on your devices and will have you choose three people to hold you accountable. You can add it to your computer, phone, or other devices.*

YOU'LL BE HAPPY YOU DIDN'T QUIT

"But as for you, be strong and do not give up, for your work will be rewarded."
—2 Chronicles 15:7

There will be plenty of opportunities for you to quit. Don't start now. The more you quit, the easier it becomes to miss out on the opportunities God has laid out for you. You may not want to continue school when it gets hard; you may want to quit the team if you don't get to start; you may want to quit on your family because of the dysfunction. I know it's tough. I've been there.

I quit football my sophomore year of high school. I was burned out because I had been playing football since I was six years old—but part of the issue was that I was playing on a losing team. I missed out on the supernatural strength and lessons that God wanted to equip me with because I took the easier way out. The following year I came back and still had to go through the teaching and growing pains in order to be equipped for the next season.

God wants you to stay strong, endure, and not give up. Your perseverance and endurance will be rewarded. God knows you can handle the challenge. If you trust in him and the process, you will see the rewards God has in store for you.

REFLECT:
Is there any situation in your life that you want to quit prematurely?
Is this situation detrimental to your health or well-being? If not, ask God
for the strength and grace to push through.

NO ROOM FOR EXCUSES

For the Spirit God gave us does not make us timid, but gives us power, love and self-discipline.
—2 Timothy 1:7

Why haven't you cleaned up your room yet? You'll do it later. How did you forget to take the trash out? You were tired from school. Why haven't you been going to your workouts? You just didn't feel like it. These are the questions you'll get when you don't follow through on a task. And when you have only excuses to offer, you show a lack of self-discipline to meet your responsibilities.

The truth is, yes, you will make mistakes. We all do. But God did not make us fearful or weak. He made us powerful. It's been said that Paul gave a similar pep talk to young Timothy in this Scripture to excite the gift of God within him.

This is for you: There should be no more room for excuses. Instead, channel a spirit of power and confidence that you are who God says you are—a pillar of strength with the spirit of God pulsating through your veins—one who isn't timid or lazy but has love and self-discipline.

REFLECT:

In what areas do you notice yourself using excuses? Next time this happens, own your mistake or shortcoming instead and make a commitment to have better follow-through next time.

HIT PAUSE

One of the greatest skills you can possess alongside humility is patience. Patience requires the mental and spiritual dexterity to wait until you have a good perspective. It's one thing if your mom tells you to be patient and you do it with a salty attitude. It's different when you reflect the beauty of patience by waiting with a positive outlook. We have opportunities almost every day to fine-tune this skill.

I know you want to grow up faster, get taller, get jacked, drive, graduate from high school, go to college, get married, have sex. None of these desires are bad in the right context or season of life, but they do require patience. You have to experience life the way God created it for you.

God's Word says that if there are things you hope for but can't yet see, you should wait patiently. Don't wait with a bitter attitude; wait with a joyful disposition. If you could see the outcome, you wouldn't need hope or faith, which means you wouldn't need God.

Think about how patient God is with you every day.

REFLECT:

What situations have you been impatient about? Write them down. Watch how God will reveal himself to you in these situations with time.

DIFFERENT IS COOL

Everybody knows that kid or group of kids at school who seem to go through life a step differently from everyone else. You may even be thinking, *Hey that's me!* If that is you, picture my hand coming through the page to give you a high five. Different is cool! If only we could get everybody to appreciate each other's differences, middle school, high school, and the world would be much more pleasant.

The Bible wants us to know that we should love each other—including people we don't know, the kids at school we don't hang out with, the new kid, the less fortunate, and even those with whom we don't see eye to eye. Remember, you never know whom you're talking to. They could be the next president, the next billionaire CEO, or—just as importantly—the next troubled human being who needs your kindness.

Keep your eye out for those who might be marginalized or treated unfairly because of who they are. There's nothing wrong with having a close group of friends—but instead of being exclusive, try to be inclusive.

REFLECT:

At any time in your life, you could be the person who needs acceptance. If you are in a place to help others feel accepted, reach out to them. It's a godly and loving thing to do and a blessing to others. Ask God to reveal to you the people who need your love and acceptance.

THE REALITY OF BULLYING

"Be strong and courageous. Do not be afraid or terrified because of them, for the Lord your God goes with you; he will never leave you nor forsake you."

—Deuteronomy 31:6

According to the National Center for Educational Statistics, more than one in five students report being bullied. Forms of bullying include teasing, taunting, threats, sexual misconduct, spreading rumors, excluding people, physical attacks, and much more. The reality of bullying is that it alienates and strips others of their wholeness. The pain, ridicule, belittling, and emptiness can drive the victim to a place of solitude and despair. This is a dangerous place.

If you are verbally, mentally, or physically bullied, you may be tempted to retaliate. I want to urge you to not give in to the vicious cycle. When you treat evil with evil, you only add to the hurt that was done to you.

I encourage you to keep Deuteronomy 31:6 permanently in your heart. Be strong and courageous; do not hide. Stand up to the bully by taking the information to authorities, teachers, principals, parents, or leaders. Lay fear down at God's feet and put on the confidence of the Lord, knowing that he is by your side every step of the way. You are not alone.

REFLECT:

If you are being bullied, tell an authority figure right away. Make sure you get help.

If you find yourself bullying others, please stop! Apologize to the person you've bullied, ask for forgiveness, repent to God, and then get help.

WHO IS YOUR PROVIDER?

"So do not worry, saying, 'What shall we eat?' or 'What shall we drink?' or 'What shall we wear?' For the pagans run after all these things, and your heavenly Father knows that you need them. But seek first his kingdom and his righteousness, and all these things will be given to you as well."

—Matthew 6:31–33

What do you need? Sure, there are different degrees of how good you may have it in comparison to your peers, but ask yourself: Are your needs met? If not, do you know who your provider is? You may be thinking, *Well, since this is a Christian devotional, you must be talking about God.* That's true, but do you know God personally? Do you have a personal relationship with him? Because if you knew who my God is, you would know Jehovah Jireh, which means "the Lord will provide."

God knows you need clothes, shoes, school supplies, healing, and food to eat next week. Matthew 6:31–33 explicitly says not to worry about any of these things. God knows what you need.

You may be asking yourself, *Will I get a car when I get my license? Will my dad land that new job? Will we have enough money to pay for my uniform?* Take it to God, pray, and leave it in his hands. Prayer gives you the strength to persevere through your daily trials and the faith to know your Father will provide.

REFLECT:
Is there anything you wish you had right now? Ask yourself how important it is, really.
Pray for God to provide what you need and leave it in his hands.

STREAMING, MOVIES, AND GAMING

"The eye is the lamp of the body. If your eyes are healthy, your whole body will be full of light.
But if your eyes are unhealthy, your whole body will be full of darkness. If then the light
within you is darkness, how great is that darkness!"

—Matthew 6:22–23

Why does it matter what I watch or allow myself to consume visually? It's just a TV show. I'm just playing a video game. I couldn't stand hearing my friends talk about a movie or show that I wasn't allowed to watch. They would quote lines, and I would do my best to play along, just so I could fit in. Now I realize how ridiculous that was. My parents had good reason to protect me from watching certain violent movies and crude shows.

They knew that "the eye is the lamp of the body." If your eyes are healthy, your whole body will be full of light. Your eyes are the gateway to your heart and soul; you must be careful about what you let in. If you let in dark, sexually explicit, or demonic images, they can corrupt the body and dim the light within you.

When you limit what you watch, you can keep your spirit clear, clean, and illuminated so that you can become the light God called you to be. You are set apart.

REFLECT:
Are there shows, movies, or games that may be assaulting your spirit? If so, I challenge you to ask God and a spiritual adviser if you should eliminate them. It may seem small, but a drop of red dye can change the color of an entire bottle of water. Keep your bottle clear.

FAMILY MATTERS

Listen, my son, to your father's instruction and do not forsake your mother's teaching. They are a garland to grace your head and a chain to adorn your neck.

—Proverbs 1:8–9

The buzzer goes off. That's the game. We just lost the first game of the high school season by two points. All I can think about is where it went wrong. The truth about me is that I hate to lose more than I like to win. Losing is brutal to the ego and daunting to your spirit. And it only gets worse when the commentary starts flowing.

When I come out of the locker room and greet my parents, my mother says, "Good game, son." I hesitate but say through clenched teeth, "Thanks, Mom." My dad shakes my hand with his *I'll talk to you later* face. I appreciate that because he knows I just need some time to unwind. But my mom doesn't notice. She starts to talk about what I could have done differently. I know she means well, but the timing's too much. I snap at her, breaking my hard-won composure, disrespecting my mom, and disappointing myself.

Of course, I apologized. But I remember this vividly because my parents did not tolerate that type of behavior. God doesn't tolerate it either. Our parents' teachings enhance and add value to our lives. My mom was doing exactly what I was doing—mentally replaying the game so I wouldn't make the same mistake twice. She knew I hated to lose, and she did nothing wrong—I did.

We must honor our parents and never take their wisdom for granted. If you respect and appreciate your family, it will shape you for life.

REFLECT:
Have you disrespected or taken your parents for granted recently? If so, apologize and ask them for forgiveness.

YOUR EMOTIONS ARE REAL

A time to weep and a time to laugh, a time to mourn and a time to dance.
—Ecclesiastes 3:4

There will be moments in your life when your emotions will change quicker than you can keep up. This does not mean you are weird or strange. It means that you are a human being with real feelings. In Ecclesiastes it says there is a time to weep, a time to laugh, a time to mourn, and a time to dance. You are not weak because you choose to show different emotions. There is actually strength in feeling your feelings and exercising balance.

Shedding tears is completely normal. Being able to let your guard down and leap with joy is medicine to your soul. When you lose someone dear to you, you need to grieve and mourn.

You have a lot on your adolescent plate. Friendships, romantic relationships, stress, worldly influences, struggles, triumphs, hormones —all of these things will spark emotions in you. Without having God in your life, it could be a vicious battleground. I want you to know that God is here for you! He loves you for who you are! Don't ever try to bury your emotions. Your emotions are real.

REFLECT:

Write out two categories. I want to help you see your emotions.
First category: what makes you feel sad
Second category: what makes you happy
Recognize these emotions, allow yourself to feel them, and embrace them.

GIVE OF YOUR TIME AND YOUR HEART

Whoever is kind to the poor lends to the LORD, and he will reward them
for what they have done.

—Proverbs 19:17

Generosity is the quality of being kind. It's like a muscle—you can work to build it up. Think about toddlers playing: The kid who shares with everyone sticks out like neon yellow against a black background. Because most toddlers don't like to share, they will scream at the top of their lungs if someone takes a toy away. But they can learn—and so can you.

God wants us to be generous with our lives. All aspects of our lives don't belong to us. They belong to the Lord. So why be stingy with things we don't own? Once you develop the habit of being generous and giving of your time and heart, it becomes addicting. Proverbs 19:17 is about having compassion and giving voluntarily in your heart. Not because you are told to or feel like you have to. If you give your friend clothes, money, shoes, video games, or even your time, make sure that your heart is aligned with God's. This means you give because you want to be generous, not because you have to be.

REFLECT:
Write down how you can be more generous at home, at school, in your neighborhood, and overall as a person.

GET ORGANIZED—IT MATTERS

Teach us to number our days, that we may gain a heart of wisdom.
—Psalm 90:12

Organization is biblical. To create this world, God was strategic—there was order to the overall plan. A man of God by the name of Moses wrote Psalm 90:12 and prayed on it daily.

What this prayer teaches us is that when we look at the big picture and realize that our days on earth are short, we understand that we need to maximize every day. You are blessed to be able to carry out the plan of God. With this responsibility, you need godly wisdom to organize and prioritize your life so you can be effective every day you are breathing!

REFLECT:
Follow in Moses's footsteps and pray on this Scripture to learn how to organize your days.
As an exercise, write down your week in columns from Monday to Sunday. To the left of the columns, write down the times of the day and what you will do each day in a week. Plan out your week, then own that plan.

I wish that all of you were as I am. But each of you has your own gift from God;
one has this gift, another has that.

—1 Corinthians 7:7

It's okay to be a beast in the gym, in the classroom, on the court, or on the mic, but whatever you do, don't wake up one particular beast before its time. The type of beast I'm talking about is lust—and it can consume you and lead you down a dark path. If you can exercise patience for the right season of your life, you will be glad you waited. There are different seasons of life, and you want to be sure to appreciate each one.

One season is that of being single (not married), which applies to most of you. It's a season that's meant to be enjoyed. You have a different type of freedom right now than you will have in later seasons. In 1 Corinthians 7:7 Paul was answering questions from the Corinthians regarding sex. I believe he was telling them, "I really wish you guys could be like me and not obsess over sex and just appreciate being single."

If you can't control yourself and feel like you are going to give in to sex, you are better off getting married. Not everyone can be like Paul, but you can do your best to not put yourself in situations that wake up the beast before its time. If you skip into the next season too early, you will eventually catch yourself regretting that you took the season you were once in for granted.

REFLECT:

Remind yourself to be patient and not rush or give in to youthful lust.
Enjoy the pros of being single in your youth. Save sex and sexual acts
for marriage.
Repeat 1 Corinthians 7:7 daily as a reminder.

WORRY LESS; BELIEVE MORE

When I am afraid, I put my trust in you.
—Psalm 56:3

Why do we worry so much? Part of the reason is that we want to be in control of situations. You probably want to make a good impression on your teachers, your crush, your coach, and your friends. You may worry about making the team, getting into your top-choice college, or growing up to be successful. These are all valid concerns—but you should not try to deal with them alone.

Putting this pressure on yourself will do you more harm than good. When it becomes overwhelming and scary, God wants you to put your trust in him, not yourself. He is the author of your book, and your life has already been written. He can lead you in wisdom.

When you feel anxiousness creeping in, I want you to read Philippians 4:6: "Do not be anxious about anything, but in every situation, by prayer and petition, with thanksgiving, present your requests to God." Say it out loud and use it as a weapon against worry. Believe more in the power of God and worry less about the current situation.

REFLECT:

What are you worrying about right now?
Write your worries on a piece of paper and let God know you are turning your troubles over to him. Then throw the paper away.

*Fathers, do not exasperate your children; instead,
bring them up in the training and instruction of the Lord.*
—Ephesians 6:4

You are to honor your parents and abide by their wisdom. With that said, you aren't supposed to experience physical, mental, or verbal abuse at the hands of anyone.

My friend in high school was a bright light to many people. She contained an inner beauty that radiated through her, impacting everyone she encountered. One day I noticed that she was smiling, talking, joking, praying, and reading her Bible less. Something felt off, and she became withdrawn. Later I found out that her father was physically, sexually, emotionally, and verbally abusing her.

Ephesians 6:4 explicitly mentions fathers, but it pertains to mothers and any authority figure. It warns parents not to be too hard on children and instead lead them to God. Sometimes your parents may have to ground you or not spare the rod for your benefit. But you do not have to put up with abuse.

You should not be provoked, wrongfully blamed, or victimized by someone's temper. Instead you should be nurtured, trained, encouraged, and disciplined in love when needed. That's what Ephesians 6:4 is saying.

REFLECT:
*If you are being abused, please get help.
Talk to an adult you trust at your school or church.
Call 911 or a crisis hotline. The Childhelp National Child Abuse Hotline
is open 24 hours a day, seven days a week, at 1-800-4-A-CHILD
(1-800-422-4453).*

Walk with the wise and become wise, for a companion of fools suffers harm.
—Proverbs 13:20

He planned on getting a full-ride basketball scholarship to a Division 1 university. He had excellent grades and was well-liked. The only problem was peer pressure; like an oil spill on his path, it caused him to slip up once in a while. He didn't initially drink alcohol, but after being teased about it, he gave in and started to drink.

Drinking and hanging out with the wrong crowd started to negatively influence his decisions. The changes were subtle but made a difference: Instead of going the extra mile to practice on his own time, he would party and get drunk. I'm not saying that you can't have fun, but know that your choices matter and the people you let into your inner circle will influence you. If you touch a hot iron, you will get burned.

Use wisdom when choosing the friends you hang out with. And remember that you never have to do what they are doing if it doesn't align with God and your belief system. Temporary fun isn't worth risking your eternal destination. Let God be the standard in your life, and allow your influence to raise the standards of your peers.

REFLECT:
Are you making poor decisions due to peer pressure and bad influences? Ask God to give you the strength to not give in to peer pressure and to show you right from wrong.

YOU ARE NOT MEANT TO DO LIFE ALONE

Every day they continued to meet together in the temple courts. They broke bread in their homes and ate together with glad and sincere hearts, praising God and enjoying the favor of all the people. And the LORD added to their number daily those who were being saved.

—Acts 2:46–47

I understand occasionally wanting to have your alone time—that's completely understandable. But when you go through tough times, you need others to talk to and help lift your spirits. You need support to navigate life's ups and downs. It is important to have friends and family showing up to your games, events, and recitals—and being by your side when tragedy strikes.

Small groups and Bible studies are awesome for the quality of your life here on earth. Going to church on the weekends is amazing, but your spiritual walk doesn't stop there. This passage from Acts shows the beautiful conception of the church community. It's simple: they spent time together and ate great food—just as you can spend more time in a community setting with friends, eating pizza, worshipping God, and studying the Bible.

REFLECT:

What group of believers or community group could you join?
Who is a source of strength and support for you?
Who can you be a source of strength for?

TURN AND RETURN

"Produce fruit in keeping with repentance."
—Matthew 3:8

My brother and I used to make crossbows with rubber bands and sharpened sticks. We had so much fun shooting them and seeing who could launch theirs the farthest. Then we started blasting each other with our makeshift weapons. Our parents told us to stop. We kept doing it—but we got caught plenty of times. Each time I would ask God for forgiveness for not obeying my parents' orders, but I didn't have true intentions of repenting.

Scripture instructs us to produce fruit in keeping with repentance—meaning your actions should represent those of someone who truly repents. *Repent* means "to turn or return." When you truly repent, you demonstrate a new behavior and change of heart—you turn from evil to good and discard any desire to commit that sin again.

One day my brother and I were in the back seat and up to no good. Before my brother could indulge in his sneaky ways, I took my crossbow and opened it up like I was going to pierce him at close range. One problem: The band slipped through my fingers, and it shot off and hit the window, then impaled him right above his eye. I felt horrible.

If I'd had a repentant heart at the time, I wouldn't have disobeyed my parents and almost taken out my brother's eye.

REFLECT:
What are you doing that you need to repent for? How will you turn away from that sin and toward a new behavior that reflects your repentant heart?
Ask God for forgiveness and help in applying the real meaning of repentance.

THE CENTER OF THE PIE

I have been crucified with Christ and I no longer live, but Christ lives in me. The life I now live in the body, I live by faith in the Son of God, who loved me and gave himself for me.

—Galatians 2:20

One of my favorite desserts is fresh-baked pie. I love the texture of a crunchy exterior and a gooey middle. When I look at a pie after it has been cut into slices, I picture a life with Jesus. The pie represents you as a person, and each slice is a different area of your life. The slices might represent family, school, sports, youth group, band, or friendships.

The gooey goodness in the middle represents Jesus. Each slice of the pie has that gooey goodness. Galatians 2:20 tells us that when you live for Christ, you no longer live by your standards. Christ becomes the center of your life because he lives within you. Jesus should be in the center of your sports life, your school life, and your social life. You should not act differently in different areas of your life; the center should always hold firm.

REFLECT:
Are there any slices of your life where Jesus Christ is not at the center? If so, ask God to make you aware of this and give you the strength to change it.
Life is easier when you are consistent in every area.

YOU CAN'T ALWAYS BE RIGHT

Everyone knows that person who always has to be right, like the kid at lunch who will argue until he wears you out and you finally agree so that you can at least eat for five minutes. That person may even be you, though you hate to admit it. But there is good news: You are not alone. Many of us struggle with pride. It's only human.

Isaiah 2:12 talks about the proud and lofty—those who think they are above everyone else—because God hates the proud. Pride caused an angel to become the devil. I'll tell you right now: I don't want to be judged by God for pride. There will be a day of judgment when God will show the proud who is boss. I'm not trying to scare you. I'm shedding light on reality.

If you can't receive correction, that's displeasing pride.

If you can't apologize when you are wrong, that's displeasing pride.

If you get upset when you are wrong, that's displeasing pride.

You can't always be right, and that's okay—understanding this is the beginning of peace.

REFLECT:
Write about a time when you let your pride get the best of you. How did you act? What did you say? Think about ways you can handle this differently.

THE BIBLE IS YOUR CHEAT SHEET

The one who gets wisdom loves life; the one who cherishes understanding will soon prosper.
—Proverbs 19:8

What if you had a big test coming up, and you were allowed to use a cheat sheet? I'm sure you would jump at the chance to have that sheet help you.

That's exactly what the Bible is to your life. It's a cheat sheet of 66 books of God's wisdom. Proverbs 19:8 says that if you receive wisdom and understanding, you will prosper.

Wisdom guides you to think twice about responding to your parents rudely, mouthing off to a coach, disrespecting the opposite sex, or belittling your siblings. Wisdom will help you through tough decisions. The Bible's wisdom can bring about holy conviction and spare your life. Wisdom is more precious than a diamond.

REFLECT:

Read a Proverbs chapter every day of the month. There are 31 proverbs, so if you are in a month with 30 days, read two chapters on the thirtieth. Meditate on the wisdom of each chapter.

HOW TO RESPOND TO CHANGE

"Have I not commanded you? Be strong and courageous. Do not be afraid; do not be discouraged, for the LORD your God will be with you wherever you go."

—Joshua 1:9

The weather changes, seasons change, people change—the transitions adolescence entails are nothing new to God. He wants you to know that he will be with you through these changes every step of the way. When your heart feels heavy, confusion starts to set in, and you feel lost, do not be afraid. Lift your head up and choke discouragement with faith and prayer.

You are young, but you have a strength that others don't have because you have Jesus in your life. You are tapped in to the source. When you are weak, his strength is your substitute. Reach out and tag him in. You can trust that God has a plan for your life, and in this time of transition he will reveal his purpose and show you the direction to go.

Do me a favor and don't miss the lessons God wants to teach and show you. "There is a time for everything and a season for every activity under the heavens" (Ecclesiastes 3:1).

REFLECT:

If you are going through big changes, have faith that God has your best interests in mind. When you feel your emotions wanting to take over, tell yourself, "God is in control." That's how you respond to transition. Ask God to reveal his plans for you in this season of your life.

IT IS ALWAYS BETTER TO FORGIVE

Bear with each other and forgive one another if any of you has a grievance against someone. Forgive as the Lord forgave you.

—Colossians 3:13

You must forgive, no matter what. But it is so much easier said than done. What do you do when someone hurts a family member? How do you forgive when a bully won't leave you alone?

I have seen young men struggle with forgiveness in many situations: *I don't want to forgive my stepdad for hitting my mom. I'm trying to forgive my mom for breaking up our family by cheating on my dad. I am hurt, and I don't feel like forgiving my uncle for stealing money from our house.*

Those are real issues, and I know forgiveness isn't always easy. But life isn't easy all the time. I want you to picture Jesus being ridiculed and forced to walk the streets with his back ripped open, carrying a wooden cross on exposed flesh. Being beaten and spit on, yelled at, and hung on the cross in the most inhumane way for something he didn't do. Yet even he had to forgive.

Colossians 3:13 requests that we bear with each other and forgive one another. We sin, make mistakes, treat people badly—on purpose and by accident—all the time. We expect God to forgive us. How can we not give the same courtesy to others? We are to forgive as the Lord has forgiven and continues to forgive.

REFLECT:
Whom do you need to forgive?
Take your time and think about it, and when you're ready,
forgive that person.
It will set you free.

BITE YOUR TONGUE

My dear brothers and sisters, take note of this: Everyone should be quick to listen, slow to speak and slow to become angry.

—James 1:19

How many times have you been in an argument and it escalated because you were not listening to each other? If you are anything like me, you are so intent on getting your point across that you either interrupt or—even worse—just wait for your turn, rather than listening and then responding appropriately.

Siblings, girlfriends, parents, best friends—anyone who is close to you on a deeper level can get under your skin and set you off quickly. If you have a temper, this piece of Scripture can truly help you: Just be willing to hold it in your heart and apply it to your life daily. James is asking everyone to be quick to listen rather than quick to speak.

With this wisdom you can have a clear head versus a hot head because you are able to hear the other side of the story and respond in an intelligent and humble way. This helps defuse anger and can even reveal to the other person how silly and illogical they are being. The next time you are in a heated discussion, remember to take a deep breath and consciously think about James's words. Hear the other party out and wait for your turn to respond.

REFLECT:
Take your time and read James 1:19 out loud. Set it to memory.
How can you help yourself apply these words in the heat of the moment?

So then, banish anxiety from your heart and cast off the troubles of your body,
for youth and vigor are meaningless.

—Ecclesiastes 11:10

Do you feel like you worry a lot about things that you can't control? Have you been avoiding social gatherings? Are you struggling to see the positive in most situations? Do you worry excessively about how others view you? Studies show that 275 million people worldwide have an anxiety disorder. This is a real issue, and people need help. But we can't just rely on other people and professionals to solve this growing issue.

We have the ability to conquer all things through Christ, who strengthens us. You have to first want help and be tired of living life on the edge. You need the desire to live life with a God-centered mentality.

Ecclesiastes 11:10 indicates we are to remove the pain in our heart. If you let anxiety fester and try to hide it, you will become overwhelmed with worry. "Cast off the troubles of your body" means that you must take care of yourself. "For youth and vigor are meaningless" suggests that before you know it, you won't be young anymore. Make a conscious effort to remember God in everything you do at your young age. You are not too young for your anxiety to be healed by God.

REFLECT:
If you suffer from anxiety, please talk to a parent or a professional,
but don't forget to include God every step of the way.

DEPRESSION IS REAL, BUT THE LORD IS WITH YOU

"The Lord himself goes before you and will be with you; he will never leave you nor forsake you. Do not be afraid; do not be discouraged."

—Deuteronomy 31:8

Depression is a real thing, and it comes in many forms. If you aren't careful, it can slowly eat away at you. My senior year in high school, right in the middle of college recruiting, we were playing one of our rivals in football. It was a big game. At the end of the third quarter, I was tackled and at the bottom of the pile. Someone grabbed my left leg and hyperextended it, tearing the meniscus in my knee.

The doctors told me I would be out for five weeks. It was the worst news I could imagine at the time. I had surgery and was prescribed pain meds to help with the inflammation. But I was allergic to the medicine, and it caused an ulcer in my stomach, which triggered me to bleed internally. I lost a lot of blood, and I couldn't understand why I was going through all of this. I felt so lonely at the same time, but my parents kept reminding me: The Lord himself is with you during this process; he will never leave or abandon you, like your teammates did. Don't be afraid.

We need to be reminded of that when sadness, depression, and loneliness set in. At times these periods are beyond our control. The only way to overcome the helplessness is to lean on God's Word and be open with the trusted authorities in your life.

REFLECT:
Do you feel depressed?
What are you going through that's causing you sadness?
Whom can you talk to?

SIX FEET BELOW BEFORE YOUR TIME

Be alert and of sober mind. Your enemy the devil prowls around like a roaring lion looking for someone to devour.

—1 Peter 5:8

The devil was once an angel, and because of pride and wanting to be God, he was cast out of Heaven and condemned for eternity. He's already been defeated, and he is on a mission to bring as many people down with him as possible. He is cunning and relentless. He can erase your youth before you realize how gifted and useful you are for the kingdom of God.

If he can rock your faith, blur your vision, and distract you with peer pressure and drugs, he will. I know you hear about so many people your age drinking, experimenting with recreational drugs, and having harmless fun. That's what the enemy wants you to think. But it's not harmless.

Think about what Peter is saying in the Bible: "Be alert and of sober mind." You can't be sober under the influence of a substance that alters your brain—even if it's legal, even if it's "harmless" (which, let's be honest, it's probably not). We have lost too many lives to the prowling lion of drugs. In 2015, more than 52,000 people lost their lives to drug overdoses. And the number keeps rising.

Don't reside six feet below before your time. You are too precious to God.

REFLECT:

Commit to staying drug free.
If you are struggling with drug use, please reach out to your leaders to get help. You can call this drug abuse hotline 24/7: 1-800-969-2134.

HELP YOUR PEERS

"Blessed are the peacemakers, for they will be called children of God."
—Matthew 5:9

Does your school have peer mediators? These are students who sit down with other students to mediate problems between two parties. They're in a position to help others come to civil resolutions.

I'll admit, I didn't know exactly what a peer mediator was when I was asked to become one in high school, but I quickly realized it was a cool opportunity to be an extension of God's love. It also taught me practical skills for conflict resolution. You can be a peer mediator without an official assignment, too, by just trying to keep the peace among your peers.

There's always going to be a group of guys who likes to stir the pot and create chaos at school, sporting events, parties, or home. But there is a blessing waiting for those of you who work for harmony. As Matthew 5:9 says, the peacemakers will be called children of God.

Your heart should not err on the side of drama, fights, and spiritual discord. With your actions, demonstrate a peaceable lifestyle. Allow God to give you divine ideas on how you can be used as a peacemaker in all areas of your life.

REFLECT:

Write down ways you can be a peacemaker at home, at school, in youth group, on the bus, at practice, on social media, and wherever you go. Start today.

CAN THEY LOOK UP TO YOU?

In everything set them an example by doing what is good. In your teaching show integrity, seriousness and soundness of speech that cannot be condemned, so that those who oppose you may be ashamed because they have nothing bad to say about us.

—Titus 2:7–8

For a while I took a group of young leaders to high school campuses. We provided food and games and sat down to share a Bible verse and ask questions about it. We did it every other week. Some kids were regulars; others came just for the food.

One student had something different about him. He was bold, not concerned about what others thought, and hungry for Jesus. He told me that he watched the way I carried myself and appreciated how I made Jesus interesting and fun. So he came to check out the small Bible group. Then youth group, then Sunday service, and now he is one of the leaders in this group.

Titus 2:7–8 says that in everything we should be an example "by doing what is good." Show integrity when you teach. Keep it pure, in its original form, by not adding or taking away from God's word. Keep yourself blameless and clear of trouble, so if an enemy would come against you, they would have nothing bad to say. When you do this, others will follow.

REFLECT:
How can you be a spiritual role model at your school or among your family members?

LOVE YOUR BROTHER OR SISTER

Be devoted to one another in love. Honor one another above yourselves.
—Romans 12:10

I know it can be hard to treat your siblings with kindness all the time. I get it. I have a brother, and for the most part we were the best of friends growing up. But when we weren't, you wouldn't even think we were related by the ways we would cut each other down.

We were (still are!) supercompetitive and played one-on-one basketball almost every day in our driveway. The games would often get physical, and we'd come very close to throwing blows. It's easy to be so close and familiar with your family that you forget to keep Romans 12:10 in mind. But it applies to everyone: "Be devoted to one another in love."

The Bible speaks of an endearing brotherly love because the love of siblings is special. You may yell at them in anger, but if anyone else disrespects or treats them wrongfully, then they're going to have a big problem—with you. The second part of the Scripture says to "honor one another above yourselves." This is a challenge worth accepting. Can you imagine if teenagers like you, all over this world, started at home with their siblings and then took it into neighborhoods and schools—the mission to treat everyone better than they expect to be treated?

This is an incredible selfless love. It's the love that God has for us and wants to impart to all of us.

REFLECT:
How can you show your brother or sister more honor than they show you? Are you willing to accept the challenge to treat everyone better than you are treated?

JESUS CAME TO SERVE

"For even the Son of Man did not come to be served, but to serve, and to give his life as a ransom for many."

—Mark 10:45

The world minimizes the role of a servant, but God has a unique approach to leadership. Jesus came to this earth not to rule and be served but to serve us.

The Bible teaches us that this is what true leaders look like—servants first, selfless and humble. Our stance as Christians is to have a servant's heart. A servant's heart will keep you grounded and in favor with God and man.

I won't say that this is an easy feat, but spending time with and learning about Jesus will create in you a desire to be more like him and follow in his humble ways.

REFLECT:

In what ways could you serve your friends, family, church, community, and school in a selfless way?
Write a list of selfless acts and chores that you could do to help your parents.

For where you have envy and selfish ambition, there you find disorder and every evil practice.
—James 3:16

Why does that guy have all the luck? It's not fair that he is a good student and the star player, gets all the attention, and is a nice guy on top of it all. I feel like God gave him all the gifts and talents and none to me.

Do these types of thoughts sound familiar? I'm sure you've been there at some point: jealous of what the other guy has and you don't. The truth is, it's not always fair. Some guys get acne, some don't; some are athletically coordinated, some aren't. But remember that everyone has insecurities. And jealousy is a dangerous place to be. In a state of envy, you are unstable, confused, overly sensitive, and easily irritated. You open yourself up to evil practices.

In this mind-set, your focus isn't on Jesus—it's on your perceived misfortunes, your insecurities, and the person you feel outshines you. God wants you to know that you have it good; you just might not know it yet. He has made you uniquely gifted and special. God wants you to take your focus off others and yourself and focus on him. He can reveal to you the bright star that you are and how he wants to use you in this world. That's all that matters.

REFLECT:
Have you been feeling jealous of anyone or anything recently? Open up to God and ask him to remove it from your heart and bring you peace.

"Truly I tell you, if you have faith as small as a mustard seed, you can say to this mountain, 'Move from here to there,' and it will move. Nothing will be impossible for you."

—Matthew 17:20

As kids, we tend to be much more fearless because we don't truly comprehend the consequences of our actions. You run down the stairs as fast as you can without thinking about the fact that you can fall and hurt yourself. You climb a tree without considering how you're going to get down.

My kids will often stand at the top of a ledge or staircase and see me standing in front of them, and without a doubt they'll leap and know I will catch them. They have pure faith that Daddy will protect them. Just imagine if you applied this same faith to trusting that God will take care of you.

The one thing you can rely on and know is that God loves you so much. His arms are open wide to help you. God just wants you to have faith. He'll always catch you.

REFLECT:
What do you need God to help you with?
Ask God to move this mountain, and have faith that the impossible will be possible.

LEADERS ARE READERS

Do your best to present yourself to God as one approved, a worker who does not need to be ashamed and who correctly handles the word of truth.

—2 Timothy 2:15

My grandmother was very clear with her rules. No hanging with friends after school until the homework was tackled. I don't mean swiftly done, I mean done carefully and with purpose—to the point where we had to explain what each chapter or question meant. Only then could we go outside and play. To be honest, I couldn't stand that rule—until I started to recognize its benefits for my life as a student.

Because of her influence, I was able to retain information I read and apply it to my life or memorize it and store it in my mind. These skills have helped me become successful as an adult, and they apply as much to the Bible as they do to school or work. It's imperative that we read our Bible consistently so that we can apply its teachings to life and communicate the Scriptures accurately and in a way that's pleasing in God's sight.

Second Timothy 2:15 does not just instruct you to read your Bible—it wants you to be a hard worker, to correctly handle the Word of truth. You do this through diligent study, prayer, and meditation. If you can look at your approach to studying the Bible and not be ashamed by your efforts, then you can present yourself to God as one approved.

REFLECT:
Have you been reading your Bible this way?
If not, now you know the effort it takes to read the Bible the way the Lord intends. Begin today.

NO ONE LOVES YOU LIKE GOD

For I am convinced that neither death nor life, neither angels nor demons, neither the present nor the future, nor any powers, neither height nor depth, nor anything else in all creation, will be able to separate us from the love of God that is in Christ Jesus our LORD.

—Romans 8:38–39

Love is a noun, but it's also a verb: It expresses an act. It is one thing to talk about it; it is another to demonstrate it through actions, such as the food your parents put on the table and the roof they keep over your head.

In middle school and high school, the word *love* gets tossed around like a baseball. So many people say it but don't understand its true meaning. A friend may have love for you—as long as you guys get along. If you guys disagree, things may change. That demonstrates conditions within the relationship, which is not healthy love.

God loves you when you are spending time with him praying, worshipping, and studying. God loves when you follow the lifestyle he wants for you. But he knows you are human, and when you slip up, he won't disown you. God isn't a flip-flopper; his love is the same yesterday, today, tomorrow, and forever. Your mistakes can't remove God's love; your bad days can't remove God's love; your bad decisions can't remove God's love; your past, your present, and future can't remove God's love. How amazing for you!

REFLECT:
Do you feel unloved right now?
Ask God to reveal his love for you. Remember that it is always there.

YOU ARE A MASTERPIECE

Your eyes saw my unformed body; all the days ordained for me were written in your book before one of them came to be. How amazing are your thoughts concerning me, God! How vast is the sum of them!

—Psalm 139:16–17

It's so easy to let other people dictate and tell us who we are. Your friends can tell you how awesome your haircut looks, and the compliment fuels you and subconsciously defines your worth. However, out of those same lips, they could make fun of you for the shirt that you wore another day or mock the size of your biceps.

It can be brutal, and unfortunately it doesn't stop with your peers. Society also does a number on us, telling us how we're supposed to be. The culture tries to define what's attractive, intelligent, cool, acceptable, and successful. The problem is that it changes often. One day baggy jeans are in; the next day it's skinny jeans. All of this is exhausting and harmful to your confidence as a person.

That's why it's beneficial to know who you are from the inside out. Not what people tell you, not what social media expects of you, but who you really are, from the architect who created you. You were intricately designed. There wasn't one mistake made when you were assembled. No one can change who you are meant to be. You are a masterpiece!

REFLECT:

Psalm 139: 16–17 is revitalizing. Write this Scripture and hang it on your wall or mirror, and read it every day.

"You shall not covet your neighbor's house. You shall not covet your neighbor's wife, or his male or female servant, his ox or donkey, or anything that belongs to your neighbor."
—Exodus 20:17

If you can be honest with yourself, at some point you wanted something that belonged to someone else. It could have been their gaming system, shoes, car, house, position on the sports team, girlfriend, or even lifestyle. It all stems from comparison. You walk past the guy at the mall with sick kicks on and automatically downgrade the pair you have.

There's nothing wrong with appreciating someone's lifestyle, but it becomes sin when you say, "I want it to be mine." God doesn't take this lightly; in fact it's one of the Ten Commandments in the Bible. You shall not covet. It's not that you can't desire or want healthy and positive things in your life. But when you find yourself losing control of your desire for what others have, it crosses over into sin.

If you are never satisfied with what you have and always craving what you don't have, you will be unhappy. Learn to be content in God. If he provides, then that's great. If he doesn't provide, then that's great. God knows what's in your best interest.

REFLECT:
Is there anything that you are coveting that someone else has?
Write it down, then release it to God and ask him to give you a heart
for contentment.

DON'T GIVE UP

Let us not become weary in doing good, for at the proper time
we will reap a harvest if we do not give up.

—Galatians 6:9

It's hard to live a consistent life—maybe you do well for a while and then fall off. But this is a vicious cycle that will ultimately lead to unfulfilled dreams. Some of you want to go to college; others would like to start businesses; others already have their dream jobs in mind. All of these goals are attainable, but if you quit, there is no one to blame but yourself.

There is a blessing that comes along with consistency. It requires you to work hard toward the goal ahead, but the power and grace of God increases your chances of finishing what you start. Let Galatians 6:9 be an anthem throughout the process. If you stay the course, you will reap the benefits of your hard work.

When you pair consistency with discipline and patience, it produces results. Work hard, be strong in your faith, and lean not on your own understanding. Let God be your coach.

REFLECT:

*What are you working on now that needs more consistency?
Take one day at a time, and ask God for the strength, grace, and patience to finish what you start.*

WHO ARE YOU BEHIND CLOSED DOORS?

I know your deeds, that you are neither cold nor hot. I wish you were either one or the other!
So, because you are lukewarm—neither hot nor cold—I am about
to spit you out of my mouth.
—Revelation 3:15–16

The way you act, talk, and treat people when you are not around your parents or other authority figures reveals your true nature. Do your actions behind closed doors sync up with how you carry yourself in public?

I remember trying to act cool in middle school. The cool kids were cursing and cracking crude jokes, and I knew better—that wasn't how I was raised or who I was. At home I would act one way with my parents, but then my brother and I would play video games in the basement and curse up a storm, trying to get better at being like the other kids.

It's normal to go through these stages as we grow up, but God doesn't want us to be two different people. He doesn't want you sinning behind closed doors and playing the role of a Christian kid in public. The Bible says you are either hot or cold; if you are lukewarm, God will spit you out of his mouth as if he never knew you. I don't know about you, but that's terrifying to me. I have good news for you, though: If you confess your sins, God will forgive you.

REFLECT:

Does the real you match the public you?
If not, confess to the Lord, repent, and ask for forgiveness. Be the person
God has called you to be both in public and when no one is watching.

YOU NEED YOUR SPACE

It is good for a man to bear the yoke while he is young. Let him sit alone in silence,
for the LORD has laid it on him.

—Lamentations 3:27–28

During this time of your life, it's important to get away from the noise of your friends, siblings, phones, computers, games, tablets, and TV. I'm not saying that these things are bad, but they can be big distractions in your life.

You also need to embrace alone time with God. This period in your life is crucial to your spiritual health. Let's face it—your hormones are changing, you're passionate, energetic, and eager for the future, and you need to exercise discipline to appreciate and grow your relationship with God.

When spending alone time with a close friend or loved one, it's the same premise. You turn away from distraction to get to know them on a deeper level. God wants to have that closeness with you as well.

Make alone time with God a priority, and experience the benefits of peace, clarity, and a stronger relationship with God.

REFLECT:
Do you spend time alone with God?
Start by carving out 10 minutes of your day to dedicate to quiet time
with him.

BE GRATEFUL

Give thanks in all circumstances; for this is God's will for you in Christ Jesus.

—1 Thessalonians 5:18

It was a beautiful autumn Saturday morning in the Midwest. The air was crisp, the trees were all shades of red and orange, and there were leaf piles everywhere, inviting us to jump in. My hometown looked like a movie set as my brother and I played outside. As time went by, we knew we had to get home, so we took a shortcut and ran through a few neighborhood lawns.

One older gentleman ran out of his back door and yelled a few choice expletives our way. We turned our heads and noticed he had a long-barrel shotgun pointed directly at us. *All this for running on his grass in order to get home?* Our eyes grew wide, but we did not slow down.

Bang! We heard a thunderous crack, and I ran the fastest I've ever run until we reached home. Our hearts were racing; we were angry and confused. As upsetting as it was, I was grateful—we were alive and unhurt.

In the Bible, Paul says to give thanks in all circumstances. In every situation, good or bad, we are not just to pray but to thank God. We are to be grateful for it all: that accolade we won in school, the bad news you just got, the surprise gifts from your parents, and the mean thing someone said about you. Why? Because when you have a relationship with Jesus, you have excitement and a reward to look forward to in eternity.

REFLECT:

Are there challenges or situations you're struggling to feel grateful for? Share this with your parents or friends, and talk about how you can view life the way Paul did in 1 Thessalonians 5:18.

DIVORCE IS NEVER EASY

However, each one of you also must love his wife as he loves himself,
and the wife must respect her husband.
—Ephesians 5:33

I didn't meet my biological grandfather on my dad's side until I was
16, and the meeting was very brief. Years later he reached out again to
our family and wanted to connect with his son and grandsons. To be
honest, I wasn't sure if I cared to. He had not been in our lives, so I
didn't really feel the need to include him. Divorce was part of our
family equation and was never easy to deal with.

If you have divorce in your family, there's redemption ahead for you.
My father didn't follow in his parents' footsteps. My parents have
modeled Ephesians 5:33 in front of my siblings and me, to give us a
hope for healthy marriages. They got married in 1978, and they are
still married to this day.

Divorce doesn't make anyone a bad person, but it does have its
repercussions. God knows you're hurting, upset, sad, and feeling as if
your family is broken. I'm so sorry for your pain. It doesn't seem fair.
Just remember that during these tough times, God is there to breathe
peace into your storm, calm your raging seas, and grace your family
with forgiveness. God wants you to know he loves you and will help
you in your future to have a beautiful, long-lasting marriage.

REFLECT:
Have you been a part of a divorce?
Write down your feelings, and ask God to help mend your heart.

THERE IS CRAZY HOPE FOR YOU

*May the God of hope fill you with all joy and peace as you trust in him,
so that you may overflow with hope by the power of the Holy Spirit.*

—Romans 15:13

You don't have to continue down a solo path. When you're in trouble-some times, you may feel like you got yourself into this mess, and that means you have to get yourself out of it. That's only partially true. Everyone needs help to get out of feelings of failure, guilt, shame, and depression. If you could get out of this yourself, you would have.

Sadness can be comfortable for a while, but no one wants to stay there long term. You need someone to shed light on the importance of letting God take over your life and fill you with his supernatural hope. When you let him fill you, you will feel the overflow of hope from the Holy Spirit.

There is crazy hope for change.

There is crazy hope for you to be happy again.

There is crazy hope for you to recover from your addiction.

There is crazy hope for bullying to stop.

There is crazy hope for you to see yourself the way God sees you.

There is crazy hope for life after a breakup.

There is crazy hope for you to make a difference one day!

REFLECT:

What do you need to hope in? Add to this list of decrees and speak it over your life daily!

WHO ARE YOU?

"A good man brings good things out of the good stored up in him, and an evil man brings evil things out of the evil stored up in him."

—Matthew 12:35

Sometimes it can be tough to know who you are. You have a lot of outside influences trying to define you. One way to start figuring this out is to evaluate your character. Your character is how people view and describe you. Your character reflects the sin nature or God's nature in you. Your family, friends, and environment can play major roles in shaping your character. The most important thing is to let God develop you by humbling yourself daily and paying attention to what you let influence you.

You were designed by God, who knows you better than anyone else does. Your desire should be to know God more so that you can learn more about who you were created to be. Let God's creation within you inform your character.

REFLECT:

Write down what you know is true of your character. In what way do your actions reflect it? What are some new actions you can take to expose those around you to your character?
Before you act, base it on the Word of God.

FALL IN LOVE WITH YOUR BIBLE

Keep this Book of the Law always on your lips; meditate on it day and night, so that you may be careful to do everything written in it. Then you will be prosperous and successful.

—Joshua 1:8

The truth is that I grew up feeling like the Bible was a forced assignment to read. *Ugh! I have to read this huge book I don't understand.* That perspective hindered my desire to read the Bible. I want to help you avoid that trap and see the Bible differently. I want you to see it for its majestic, powerful, living, cinematic story. This book is literally life changing.

Start by finding a Bible translation that you can understand. This will help you engage. Then carefully read over the words, savoring them. Don't rush the reading; rather, think about what it's saying and what jumps out to you. Think about how you can apply it to your life.

Joshua 1:8 says to "meditate on it day and night." Let the Bible be an influence on your life decisions. Follow what it says, and then you will be prosperous and successful. Remember: Don't make it a "have to"— it's an exciting "get to."

REFLECT:

Schedule time to read the Bible daily. Here's my favorite way to meet with the Bible:
READ: a Scripture passage.
OBSERVE: what you just read by highlighting or circling what jumps out at you.
APPLY: Think about how you can apply this Scripture to your life now.
PRAY: Ask God to help this Scripture be a part of your day.

WATCH WHAT YOU SAY

Do not let any unwholesome talk come out of your mouths, but only what is helpful
for building others up according to their needs, that it may benefit those who listen.

—Ephesians 4:29

I once saw a college-age woman sitting next to her mom in the library. Every once in a while, she would tap her mom and say, "Did you hear those people talking?" or, "Did you hear the loud truck drive by?" Each time, her mom replied, "Yes, darling." She giggled and told her mom, "I can hear you chewing your gum." A young man walked over to their side of the table and said, "I think something is off with your annoying daughter."

The mom looked at the rude boy and said, "She just checked out of the hospital. Her surgery was a success. She was born deaf. Today is the first time she can hear sounds."

The lesson here is to guard your words. Think before you speak, and don't let judgmental or unwholesome talk come out of your mouth. Speak uplifting words and have patience. Never judge, because you never know another person's story.

REFLECT:
Have you used your words toward someone for harm? Ask for forgiveness.

CHILL OUT

"Peace I leave with you; my peace I give you. I do not give to you as the world gives. Do not let your hearts be troubled and do not be afraid."

—John 14:27

We've all had those moments when we felt as if our insides were going to burst with uncertainty. Waiting to hear back from colleges. Caught doing something you shouldn't have been doing and waiting on the verdict from the authorities. As humans, our natural response to trauma and unknowns is stress. It can be easy to succumb to stress when you don't have the strength and guidance of the Lord.

But the Bible says, "I'll give you a peace that the world can't offer you. This peace will bring you stillness during the toughest of times." When you find yourself in stressful situations, ask for this type of peace. Use the words of John 14:27 to help you in every area of your life. You could even be at the free-throw line and ask God to give you peace in the moment. He will help you chill out.

REFLECT:
What are you stressing about right now?
Ask God to give you his peace in the situation.

I SEE YOU ONLINE

*Anyone who hates a brother or sister is a murderer, and you know
that no murderer has eternal life residing in him.*

—1 John 3:15

Did you know that more than 7 percent of middle school and high school students have had mean or hurtful web pages created about them? Cyberbullying has become one of the cruelest and most cowardly things you can do. Cyberbullies take advantage of opportunities and crave attention. What might seem like a minor act online can ruin someone's life and even drive a victim to violence against himself or others.

I want you to understand that cyberbullying is a demonstration of hate, which God can't stand. His Word says anyone who hates a brother or sister is a murderer, and murderers don't get to spend eternal life with Jesus Christ. Cyberbullying is a sin—it is wicked and ungodly.

If you know of any cyberbullying taking place, stand up and take action against this brutal act of sin.

REFLECT:

Are you a cyberbully? If so, pray on 1 John 3:15, repent, and ask God for forgiveness.
If you are a victim of cyberbullying, please report it to your parents or an authority at school or church, and get help.

START YOUR DAY MOTIVATED

"For I know the plans I have for you," declares the Lord, "plans to prosper you and not to harm you, plans to give you hope and a future."
—Jeremiah 29:11

Let's face it: It can be tough to get up in the morning. It can be that much harder when you're getting up early to go to school. I used to assault my alarm clock for having the audacity to wake me up. You may not want to get up, go to school, and work hard. Some of you may lack motivation because you don't have a vision to be great or see yourself being used by God in an important way.

The fact is, you are never too young to be used by God or be the spark that motivates others. High schoolers, you are not too cool to discover what God has planned for you, which will give you a hope and bright future. Grab ahold of Jeremiah 29:11 as a constant reminder that God wants you to do great things! He needs you to be motivated every day.

REFLECT:
Write out a list of things and people that motivate you.
In prayer, ask God to motivate you with his words and by the Holy Spirit.

QUIET STRENGTH

The quiet words of the wise are more to be heeded than the shouts of a ruler of fools.
—Ecclesiastes 9:17

You may come across as quiet, reserved, or less talkative than the rest of your peers. Too many people see that as weakness in our loud, pushy world and might want to immediately label you as shy. Just because you are not boisterous or the center of attention doesn't mean you can't command respect and authority.

When Jesus is the center of your life and he rules and reigns in your heart, his power is inside of you. You possess a quiet boldness and courage. There is a saying that still waters run deep—in other words, you don't need to be loud or raging to be strong. Even if you are quiet or reserved, you can rise up against the enemy with a strength that will make demons flee. You can conquer all things through Christ, who strengthens you.

REFLECT:
If you feel shy or timid, speak Ecclesiastes 9:17 to yourself.
If someone wants to define you by calling you shy, tell them with love,
"That's not who I am."

LISTEN TO GOD'S PLANS FOR YOU

In their hearts humans plan their course, but the Lord establishes their steps.
—Proverbs 16:9

If you can learn the art of making plans and letting the Lord interrupt them, you will simplify your life. It's awesome to make plans with your family or friends; however, when you don't let God lead the course of your life, you can be misdirected on your path.

In high school I made plans with my brother to meet up with friends at a graduation party, and my parents told us not to go. We went anyway, knowing God was telling us not to. While I was partying it up, my phone rang, and my mom asked me where I was. I lied, said we were just hanging out with friends, and grabbed my brother. We jumped in the car to speed home from the other side of town. Sure enough, red and blue lights soon turned on behind me. I was going 98 miles per hour in a 45 mile-per-hour zone. So you can imagine how bad that ticket was—and how angry our parents were. When we got home, our dad was sitting on the front steps just waiting for us.

If I had listened to my parents and to God, none of that would have happened. I tried to make my own plans, but God had another plan in store for me that night.

REFLECT:
When God interrupts your plans, let him. He knows what's in your best interest.

IT'S GO SEASON

All hard work brings a profit, but mere talk leads only to poverty.
—Proverbs 14:23

I listened to an interview conducted by Pastor Steven Furtick that
helped change my approach to life. Bishop T. D. Jakes said in the
interview that there is an older version of you relying on the young you
right now. I took his words to mean that right now I can maximize my
youthful energy. It's best to accomplish the things that I have energy
to do now, before I get to an age when my energy is not so vibrant.

Proverbs 14:23 is a reminder that you don't need to tell people all
the things you are going to do; you just need to do them. You will
always gain something from hard work. If you work hard in school,
you will get good grades. If you work hard at your sport, craft, and
creativity, you will see success as a result. Work hard on that dream
God put in your heart. When no one else wants to work, remind
yourself, "I have energy for a reason. It's go season." Take advantage
of your youthful zeal. Do more working than talking now, and you
will reap the benefits.

REFLECT:
*Are there goals in your life about which you're doing more talking than
acting? Pray for the strength to focus on your actions.*
*What will the older you look back on and thank you for investing energy
in right now? Make a list of these things.*

SECONDHAND CHRISTIANITY

I love those who love me, and those who seek me find me.
—Proverbs 8:17

We're all familiar with the dangers of secondhand smoke—tobacco smoke that is exhaled by smokers and inhaled by people nearby. Non-smokers who are exposed to secondhand smoke are at a 25 to 30 percent greater risk of heart disease, according to the American Heart Association. This means that just inhaling the smoke from someone smoking around you can cause problems that can lead you away from good health and result in death.

Christianity works in the same way. If all you do is listen to other people's love for God and their own Christian talk, you will receive only what they are exhaling. That is what I call secondhand Christianity. I'm not saying the information given by your parents or pastors is wrong. What I'm saying is that God wants you to seek him for yourself. If you do receive secondhand information about God and it's wrong, it could lead you astray and ultimately take you out.

Make it a point to have your own relationship with God and get to know him and his Word for yourself.

REFLECT:

Have you experienced secondhand Christianity?
What are you doing now to know God for yourself?

BE A VISIONARY

Where there is no revelation, people cast off restraint;
but blessed is the one who heeds wisdom's instruction.

—Proverbs 29:18

Have you ever played a game of tag or capture the flag at night in pitch darkness? Without lights to guide you, you will just run around wildly trying to figure it out.

We are imperfect people, and without God's divine instructions, we will roam this earth aimlessly. Without guidance from God and the Bible, we wouldn't know when to say yes or no. When you pay attention and follow the vision God has for your life, you will experience blessings. God will highlight the desires of your heart. Knowing God's vision for you will give you clear direction.

REFLECT:
Do you have a vision for your life?
Write down your vision, and start to see yourself achieving it.
Taking a peek into the future will give you motivation in the present.

WORK WITH WHAT YOU HAVE

We have different gifts, according to the grace given to each of us.
If your gift is prophesying, then prophesy in accordance with your faith.
—Romans 12:6

I know body shaming is hurtful. In the locker room, some guys make fun of each other's bodies while changing before PE class or practice. Sometimes it's harmless, but more often than not it stings.

No matter what people say, remember that God created you differently from anyone else. You have gifts that are tailor-made for you. Your brother may be able to talk to new people nonstop for hours while you might not be graced with that kind of patience. That's okay. You need to be happy with how God has created you. You may have broader shoulders, and your best friend may have stronger abs—but as soon as you view things through the goggles of envy, you start to compare, which becomes debilitating to who you are. You don't need to look like anyone else. How boring would our world be if everyone looked the same?

Embrace your individuality, and work with what you have.

REFLECT:
Write out five things that you love about yourself.
Ask God how he will use your uniqueness.

AM I READY TO DATE?

As obedient children, do not conform to the evil desires you had when you lived in ignorance.
—1 Peter 1:14

If you have feelings for someone at school and aren't sure if it's time to start dating, I recommend you ask yourself a few questions. First, are you in a period of your life when you can get married? Do you have a job that could support you as a couple? Are you financially stable? Do you feel ready to make a real commitment?

I know some of your friends like to take the casual approach to dating because they enjoy saying they have girlfriends. But dating is serious business. You need to be prepared to take it to the next step. If you answered no to any of the above questions, it's too early for you to date.

You don't have to do what the world is doing. Your intentions should be pure and honorable. There is nothing wrong with being friends and admiring someone. However, rushing into a relationship at the wrong time could ruin a good thing. Take your time; don't rush dating.

REFLECT:
Read 1 Corinthians 13:4–5 as a bonus Scripture.

DON'T BE A SLAVE

Flee the evil desires of youth and pursue righteousness, faith, love and peace,
along with those who call on the LORD out of a pure heart.

—2 Timothy 2:22

In our culture today, there is a near-constant assault on your purity. You find sexual overtones on television, on social media, on billboards, and in magazines and some video games. As a young Christian, you are told to flee from evil youthful desires and lust, but how can you do that?

If you try to hide your desire from your parents or an authority in your life, it will become like fungus in a dark, wet place. It will continue to grow. You can't overcome lust by yourself. You need help. You need accountability. You need the Lord and his Scriptures to shower your spirit and shed light on the sin that wants to grow in darkness. First, admit your weakness—that the temptation is there but you don't want to give in and sin anymore. Remember that everyone goes through this.

Only God knows what you are thinking about. He knows if you take double and triple looks at things you know you should not look at. The thought is the root of your corruption. Kill it at the root. Pray, and then obey what God says. And seek help.

REFLECT:
Apply this devotion in your life so that you can overcome this constant battle with lust.

DON'T PUT IT OFF

Diligent hands will rule, but laziness ends in forced labor.
—Proverbs 12:24

Everybody deals with procrastination sometimes. But it can quickly become a slippery slope for your spiritual life. When we become lazy and start to put off our homework, chores, and practice, we're more likely to start putting off our relationship with God. Our Bible reading and prayer life will soon follow suit.

Hard workers will always rise to the top while those who are lazy or wait until the last minute will falter. I understand the feeling of working under pressure and how that can sometimes motivate us to finish things at the very end. But even if you can finish clutch at the buzzer, that's not a substitute for well-planned, diligent time spent on a task. When you take time to do your work well and do it in advance, you'll have better results. This skill will serve you throughout your life.

REFLECT:

Are you guilty of procrastination?
Try to write out your day the night before and plan out your deadlines ahead of time to see how it feels to be ahead of schedule.

I JUST CAN'T GET USED TO THIS

It is better to go to a house of mourning than to go to a house of feasting,
for death is the destiny of everyone; the living should take this to heart.
—Ecclesiastes 7:2

One Labor Day weekend, I lost a friend in a boating accident. Her death came as a shock—and an eye-opener. She was the life of the party, young, and still figuring out her purpose in life. No one expected this devastating news or this tragic gift.

You might ask: *How in the world is that a gift?*

Ecclesiastes 7:2 says, "It is better to go to a house of mourning than to go to a house of feasting, for death is the destiny of everyone; the living should take this to heart."

Her death forced us to mourn and think about life in the present. Death makes you hit the reset button and, for some, will help put life into perspective.

Mourning becomes a gift when it helps you pinpoint your purpose in life, especially if you've been living off track. It can wake you up and center you. Childish, insignificant actions are reevaluated during times of grief. The realization of how quickly life can change sparks a motivation to live life the way God intended you to live—which is to serve him and share the good news and expose others to a life with Jesus Christ at the helm.

REFLECT:
How does death affect you?
Be sure to share your feelings with someone you trust and allow
Ecclesiastes 7:2 to recalibrate you if needed.

PAY ATTENTION TO THE GAME

Whoever heeds discipline shows the way to life,
but whoever ignores correction leads others astray.
—Proverbs 10:17

It was rivalry week, and we traveled to our opponent's home field for the football game. Being a running back coach at the time, I was extremely amped, anticipating that my players would have a great game.

The game was close and very intense. During the third quarter, one of my running backs started to let his emotions get the best of him. He started to engage in a fight on the field, and he couldn't cool off.

No one truly wants to be corrected or told what to do, but if you can listen to discipline and correction, that is a godly thing. It will place you on a path to life. An inability to receive correction will place you on a path of destruction.

I ran onto the field, looked him in the eyes, and gave him an ultimatum: He could take control and I would keep him in the game—or he would sit out for this and the next game.

Thankfully he came to his senses, listened, and played a great game. He was able to emerge from the experience with a clear head and good spirits rather than the cloud of darkness that would have descended if I'd had to remove him.

REFLECT:

Do you have trouble listening to correction?
Think past the moment you are in and ask yourself if it's worth jeopardizing your future by not listening now.

UNDERAGE DRINKING ISN'T COOL

Let us behave decently, as in the daytime, not in carousing and drunkenness, not in sexual immorality and debauchery, not in dissension and jealousy. Rather, clothe yourselves with the Lord Jesus Christ, and do not think about how to gratify the desires of the flesh.

—Romans 13:13–14

I never drank. I was the kid who showed up to a party and my friends knew to give me ginger ale or Hawaiian Punch. Truthfully, you are not missing out. I still had lots of fun. And once it was established, once everyone knew my priorities, no one batted an eye.

The trouble with drinking is that it can be thought of as innocent, youthful fun—until something life-altering happens.

Teenage drinking has been linked to so many untimely deaths and criminal acts. The Bible tells us to obey the laws of the land. Underage drinking is breaking the law, so right away that is a red flag. Breaking the law is ungodly, not to mention risky. It can get you in real trouble.

Life can be hard at times. It comes with its ups and downs, but using alcohol to drown or ignore your pain doesn't help, because that same pain, that same issue, will be waiting for you when you get sober. It may even feel worse in the aftermath of drinking.

God does not want you filled up with alcohol, making poor decisions; he wants you filled with the Holy Spirit, making wise decisions. Being a Christian is about living a life that is pleasing to him.

REFLECT:

What are the downfalls of underage drinking? Can you commit to staying alcohol free? Meditate on Romans 13:13–14 for guidance.

BE A CHEERFUL GIVER

Each of you should give what you have decided in your heart to give, not reluctantly or under compulsion, for God loves a cheerful giver.

—2 Corinthians 9:7

Once, at our neighborhood grocery store's self-serve water dispenser, a gentleman walked up to me and asked me if I had some change so he could get something to eat. I told him, "Sorry, no, I don't." In the back of my mind I judged him, thinking he would just use it to buy alcohol. I walked up to the dispenser and realized the price had gone up by 10 cents.

I turned around to look for 10 cents in my car, and the guy walked up to me again and said, "Do you need some change for your water?" My heart sank. He reached out and gave me 10 cents and said, "God loves a cheerful giver." Ouch.

God knows our hearts; we are to give because we enjoy giving. God knows what we are capable of giving—whether it's our money, possessions, or time. We should love to bless people. We should not be reluctant.

REFLECT:
When you have an opportunity to give, take advantage of it, and do it with a cheerful heart.
What can you do to give back to your school, church, or a charity today?

YOU ARE NOT THE JUDGE

You, then, why do you judge your brother or sister? Or why do you treat them with contempt?
For we will all stand before God's judgment seat.

—Romans 14:10

He came to class with a brand-new pair of Nike Air Jordan 5s. If you are a sneakerhead, you know how cool these shoes are. The kid was sitting in the back of the class and must have been bored. He took a paper clip and opened it up until it was a straight wire, then he proceeded to puncture a hole in the air bubble at the sole of the shoe.

The thoughtless act ruined his shoes and caused a squeaky noise every time he took a step. I couldn't help but want to judge him for his actions because he took for granted what he was blessed to have! But I was reminded that I'm not the judge of anyone's activity. At the end of the day, you need to account only for what you do. The Lord will judge you for your actions—no one else's.

Think carefully about your actions and the consequences that come along with them. But don't go around judging others for their actions—that's not your job. At the end of your life, it's between you and God and no one else.

REFLECT:
Recognize when you feel the urge to judge someone for what they are doing, and shift your focus. Pay attention only to your own actions.

BICKERING BACK AND FORTH

A hot-tempered person stirs up conflict, but the one who is patient calms a quarrel.
—Proverbs 15:18

As human beings we tend to like a good argument. Some of you like to argue more than others. You may see your parents lose their cool while driving. Siblings tend to bicker back and forth. Parents may argue with each other at home about different subjects. You may have seen athletes argue with each other or their coaches.

The root of these flared tempers is a lack of satisfaction. Satan wasn't satisfied with just being an angel with a gargantuan gift in music—he wanted to be just as powerful as God. Most of the time when we argue, we want to get our point across; pride takes over our reasoning, and we stir up conflict rather than trying to calm the situation.

Arguing typically doesn't solve a disagreement—it generally elevates the discontent on each side and makes it harder to reach a solution. When we argue, it's a representation of the world absent of God. We are to represent a life with God leading us. It's so much easier said than done, but when you are about to engage in a verbal boxing match, think: *Do I want to represent a godless, hot-tempered person or a godly, patient, and calm Christian?*

REFLECT:
Do you argue a lot?
Do you have a hot temper?
Ask God to help you be calmer in difficult situations.

I AM UNASHAMED

For I am not ashamed of the gospel, because it is the power of God that brings salvation to everyone who believes: first to the Jew, then to the Gentile.

—Romans 1:16

There may be a time in your life when being a Christian isn't considered cool or popular. In the eyes of some of your peers, you may seem as foreign as an extraterrestrial. That's okay. The problem isn't with you; it's with their lack of knowledge about those you serve. Jesus was also cast out. If your peers knew the hero you served, they would not hate on you but join you in your purpose and quest to open people's eyes to truly know Jesus.

Walk with your chest out and your chin high. Be unashamed of the God you serve and the Gospel you share from the greatest book ever written this side of Heaven. God's influence on this world is unmatched. His power is unparalleled. He can meet anyone where they're at and speak healing and life into their situation. If they choose to let him rule in their lives, God has promised eternal life after this one on earth through his son Jesus Christ.

This is something to get excited about, not conceal!

REFLECT:
What has been holding you back from starting a Bible club at your school? How can you inspire others to be unashamed of their Christian faith?

IT'S NOT ALL ABOUT THE PHYSICAL

For physical training is of some value, but godliness has value for all things,
holding promise for both the present life and the life to come.

—1 Timothy 4:8

In high school, I looked in the mirror one day and noticed that my chest was getting bigger and my biceps had veins in them, and that was all the motivation I needed. I've always had a fascination with muscles and being in shape. When I was five, I did push-ups with my dad. He was in the military, and my brother and I looked up to him so much. I love health and fitness, and it's a common conversation when I talk to high school and middle school boys.

But as much as I love and dedicate myself to fitness, I love God more. Being in good physical shape has value here on this earth, but it doesn't compare to the spiritual growth that impacts your eternal life. This life here is temporary. Our final destination should be Heaven. Remember to keep the two in balance and not become too focused on the physical. God needs you to be healthy, but, more importantly, he needs you to be his servant in whatever way he deems fit.

REFLECT:
Take care of the body God gave you.
Have balance in your life.
Remember, godliness over the physical.

BODY UNDER ATTACK

Cast your cares on the LORD and he will sustain you; he will never let the righteous be shaken.
—Psalm 55:22

We tend to do silly stuff when we are young. I knew one young man who felt he was in love in middle school. His girlfriend broke up with him, and he didn't know what to do. He didn't make Jesus his source or comforter, so he acted on his emotions, which were out of control. After the tears dried up, then the anger came. He took a scalpel from bio lab, locked himself in the bathroom, and started carving into his skin. Guys, I know you will go through things during your teen years that feel major and cause you to feel helpless. But please hit pause if you find yourself going too far.

Breakups, arguments, anger, sadness, loneliness, addictions, depression—nothing is too big for God to come alongside you and shoulder the load. Psalm 55:22 reminds you to give your cares to the Lord and he will sustain you. With that type of strength in your corner, you never need to hurt yourself. Granted, things may still feel overwhelming, but you have a God who is bigger than your trials, and he is willing to go to battle by your side.

REFLECT:

Have you ever thought about hurting yourself?
If so, let your parents or an authority figure know right away, so they can get you help.

WHEN FRIENDS HURT YOU

*"For if you forgive other people when they sin against you,
your heavenly Father will also forgive you."*

—Matthew 6:14

What is the natural response to betrayal? When someone hurts a family member, friends turn their backs or people judge. Most people want to seek revenge. You might think, *How can I let someone disrespect my sister, talk down to my mother, and make fun of the clothes that I wear? This isn't right. They don't know my story, my struggle, or my pain.*

You're right—they don't know your story, and how they treat you may be completely uncalled for . . . but take a minute. Betrayal is part of life here on earth. You will feel betrayed by people you trust, and you will inadvertently betray the trust of others. Think about how imperfect everyone is, including yourself, and the mistakes you probably make without knowing you make them. If you can't forgive those who hurt you, why would you expect God to forgive you for the intentional or unintentional hurt you cause him daily?

God wants you to humble yourself and forgive those who betray you. Imagine if Jesus hadn't forgiven those who betrayed him. We wouldn't have a chance at eternal life.

REFLECT:
Have you felt betrayed by a close friend? Ask God for the strength to forgive them.
If you've betrayed the trust of someone else, ask that person humbly for forgiveness.

Accept one another, then, just as Christ accepted you, in order to bring praise to God.
—Romans 15:7

It's natural to connect with people who have interests similar to your own. You instinctively gravitate toward people who think like you and share your passions. There isn't anything wrong with having close friends. In fact, it's healthy—you need friends you can trust and be transparent and open with. The problem occurs when your group of friends alienates others. This can even be a form of bullying.

We are to accept everyone, just as Christ has accepted you. Accepting all people brings God praise. Can you be that special light that attracts all ethnicities, sizes, ages, and backgrounds? Envision the unity that you can create in your sphere of influence. You have the power to bring different people together, with the common denominator being the love of Christ. A godly life is inclusive—not exclusive.

That is a beautiful picture of being a Christian.

REFLECT:
How can you be more inclusive at school?
Try hanging out with someone new this week.

SOAK YOUR LIFE IN PRAYER

Pray continually.
—1 Thessalonians 5:17

When you are studying for a test, practicing for a recital, planning a fishing trip, or perhaps something harder, like choosing which parent to live with or responding to a friend who hurt you, pray continually. When planning your day, picking which school to attend in the fall, practicing for your speech, and putting on your uniform before the game, pray continually. This may seem like a simple piece of Scripture, but these two words—"pray continually"—have incredible depth and meaning.

Praise God for who he is. Give thanks to the Almighty and his generous, loving heart for us. You should include prayer in every area of your life. When you are having an amazing day and you feel problem-free, pray continually. When you are in the depths of despair, pray continually. God gets the glory in every aspect of your life, including the times of adversity, because God knows what's in your best interest in the end.

Prayer unlocks the door between you and him. Taking time to listen to God will change your monologue into a dialogue, which will improve your life.

REFLECT:
Try having multiple conversations throughout the day with God. Before you read your Bible, pray for revelation—for God to speak to you through his Word.

"Give, and it will be given to you. A good measure, pressed down, shaken together and running over, will be poured into your lap. For with the measure you use, it will be measured to you."

—Luke 6:38

The Bible simply asks us to give 10 percent of our earnings back to God. If you get 50 dollars for doing chores one month, then you would put five dollars in the offering plate at church. There is a blessing when we tithe; it's an act of faith.

God is telling you exactly how he wants to bless you in Luke 6:38. When he says "pressed down, shaken together and running over," he is saying he doesn't want to treat you the way some cereal companies do. Have you ever picked out your favorite box of cereal and then opened it to find there's only about half the amount you expected inside? It's filled based on weight. Once the cereal has settled, you feel cheated. If you were at Jesus's market, he would fill your box up, let it settle, press it down, shake it together, and then fill it again until it's spilling over. I don't know about you, but that's a God I want to give to.

REFLECT:

God wants to bless you. I challenge you to not miss out on your opportunity to tithe. Give your offering and see how Heaven showers blessings down on your life.

WHO'S THE FAMOUS ONE?

*"I am the vine; you are the branches. If you remain in me and I in you,
you will bear much fruit; apart from me you can do nothing."*
—John 15:5

Some of you try to avoid attention and fame like a disease. Others chase fame like a cheetah chasing down a gazelle. Some of you will experience fame as you get older. The world likes to highlight special gifts that stand out among the crowd. God gives everyone gifts, but certain gifts receive more earthly attention than others.

You may gain fame for being able to sing really well, play a sport in superb fashion, or sketch beautifully. These are gifts, but they are God's gifts to you. If you forget that the gift giver is the main focus, not the recipient of the gift, you will find yourself disconnected from the vine. If you are removed from the vine, you will no longer be able to produce godly fruit.

Always stay connected to God. I'm not asking you to be falsely humble. Authentically and genuinely funnel all attention and accolades back to God. When you are humble, you can use your gift and fame to lead people to Jesus Christ.

REFLECT:
Have you lost sight of who your fame belongs to?
How can you keep the focus on God?

INTERNET GANGSTERS

Where there is strife, there is pride,
but wisdom is found in those who take advice.
—Proverbs 13:10

Gaming online breeds a lot of verbal gymnastics. Some guys like to compete and playfully trash talk. It can be fun to outwit and throw someone off their game once in a while. But competition can quickly fuel intensified battles. It can create an unsafe environment. Cruel, racially motivated comments and threats are wrong and cross over into bullying. You need to exercise control when you are online. Always consider your safety and the safety of others. Crossing the line puts you in the sin zone.

The Bible says that where there is strife, there is pride, and pride is one of the things God hates. Take Proverbs 13:10 to heart. Don't be an Internet gangster; don't try to intimidate or belittle. It's all too easy to act differently online than you would in person. Be smart, and don't engage with verbal brutality. It's not cool. It's better to log off, cool down, and turn your focus to the positive.

REFLECT:
Use wisdom when you engage with people online. Safety comes first. If you are a bully online, stop trying to create strife, because it's rooted in ungodly pride.

FROM DISAPPOINTMENT TO ENCOURAGEMENT

And we know that in all things God works for the good of those who love him, who have been called according to his purpose.

—Romans 8:28

Disappointment will visit you from time to time. Your parents, friends, coaches, teachers, bosses, siblings, and country will let you down occasionally. How you respond to disappointment determines your success. You have limited strength, and God doesn't have any weakness. I can give you a spiritual hack that lies within Romans 8:28: If you believe and know that God will work all things out for good, you will find peace.

God provides the safety so that you don't get discouraged; he gives you confidence by helping you recognize that you are not in this alone. Think about one of the hardest situations you had to get through recently and how God helped deliver you. God's words are unchanging; if he did it before, he will do it again.

REFLECT:

What are you disappointed about right now?
Take time to share it with a parent, authority figure, or friend and then pray for God to give you supernatural peace and show you that it will work out for good. Be encouraged.

Flee from sexual immorality. All other sins a person commits are outside the body, but whoever sins sexually, sins against their own body.

—1 Corinthians 6:18

"Don't have sex before marriage!" That's all you hear as a Christian. It provokes more questions: *What's the big deal? So, if I don't have sex before marriage, am I fine to do other things? What does "sexual immorality" even mean?*

Sexual immorality is a surrendering of sexual purity. It describes any type of sexual act that isn't within the confines of a God-ordained marriage. I know people in this world don't abide by these wise words—and unfortunately, it's very apparent when you hear about sexually transmitted diseases, early pregnancies, and heartbreak. God isn't telling you this because he wants to take something from you. He is giving you a gift. Saving sex until marriage is biblical and blessed. Sex outside of marriage is fornication and sexually immoral, even if it involves safety precautions.

God wants you to be set apart from the world and its way of operating. The big picture is for your safety here on earth and for you to have eternal life beyond this one.

REFLECT:

Don't be pressured into having premarital sex. The temporary pleasure isn't worth the long-term repercussions.

Have you had premarital sex? If so, you can repent, ask for forgiveness, and wait for marriage from here on out.

NO ONE HAS A MIND LIKE YOU

Do you see someone skilled in their work?
They will serve before kings; they will not serve before officials of low rank.
—Proverbs 22:29

God created you this way. Not everyone has a mind like you. Not everyone can build things with their hands, put together words, shoot photos, speak, sing, dance, read, memorize, design, or do anything quite like you do. In the beginning of time, God created the blueprint for this world with creativity interlaced with wisdom.

Look into the mirror and see how creative God is: You are unlike anyone or anything on this planet. Don't take your skills for granted. Make sure to develop and perfect your craft with diligent hard work. The Bible says those who are skilled in their work will serve before kings. Diligence is rewarded with success. I know you are young and you want to enjoy life. I'm not saying you can't have fun, but I want to encourage you to be diligent with your craft because your creativity, skills, and gifts will lead you to walk through open doors.

REFLECT:

What are you creatively gifted in?
Write down your gifts, and start to work on becoming better in your skill set.

COMPLY AND STAY ALIVE

"If you are willing and obedient, you will eat the good things of the land."
—Isaiah 1:19

I have to remind my little kids to not run out into the street. I tell them constantly to stop running in the house, not to play with sharp utensils, and to quit jumping from the stairs when Mommy and Daddy aren't around to catch them. I'm not telling them these things because I want to restrict them and have them live life wearing bubble wrap. I impart these instructions for their safety. I know what's best for them.

And God knows what's best for you. He gave us a book of guidance and help from the Holy Spirit to lead us in the way we should go. The Bible says that if you are willing to be obedient, you will eat of the good things of the land, meaning that you will receive many blessings on this earth. Obedience can save your life, guard you from the enemy's attacks, bring blessings to your family, and make your path easier.

REFLECT:
Do you struggle with obeying?
If so, strive to know and obey God.

My son, do not forget my teaching, but keep my commands in your heart, for they will prolong your life many years and bring you peace and prosperity. Let love and faithfulness never leave you; bind them around your neck, write them on the tablet of your heart. Then you will win favor and a good name in the sight of God and man.

—Proverbs 3:1–4

Favor means achieving validation or special benefits or blessings. We show favor to people who treat us well or like us. The teacher who shows you favor probably recognizes that you listen to them and respect them. When you feel that love and affection from others, you tend to give them favor as well. God's favor shines on you when you show him love with your life and respond completely to his call for you.

There was a boy in the Bible named Joseph who found favor with the Lord because he surrendered his life for God. Surrendering your life for God comes with a price—you can't be like everyone else, you can't do all the things everyone else does, and you must stay focused. But if you do this, you will become set apart for a higher purpose. If you want the favor of the Lord on your life, follow what Proverbs 3:1–4 says.

REFLECT:
Read about Joseph and his inspiring favor in Genesis 37:1–44:9. Meditate on the Scripture, and think about how you can find favor with the Lord.

"Everyone who is called by my name, whom I created for my glory, whom I formed and made."
—Isaiah 43:7

You are much more than a student, brother, son, best friend, athlete, musician, or artist. The intricacies and attention to detail it took to craft such a magnificent version of you is incomparable. You were designed in the image of God. For you to figure out your purpose on this earth, you must first know that you were created for God's glory and give him glory with your life.

Take what God infused in you and use it to give glory to him, not for your own gain. This is your true purpose: to shed light on how God can use you to open people's hearts to him. When you live for your own selfish aims, you miss out on the endless possibilities that God has for you. Our selfishness stagnates us and gives us a basic outlook on life. Imagine looking at an old-school black-and-white TV—that represents your gain. When God is at the foreground of your life, the picture bursts with color, more vivid than anything you've ever experienced.

REFLECT:
To find your purpose, remember why you were created: for God's glory. This will give you the foundation for your life.

CLEAR CUT

Search me, God, and know my heart; test me and know my anxious thoughts. See if there is any offensive way in me, and lead me in the way everlasting.
—Psalm 139:23–24

There are a few reasons why diamonds are so special. One is the fact that they can last forever. Another is that when a diamond is cut right, it radiates a beautiful brilliance. If you have a low-quality or poorly cut diamond, it looks cloudy, and when light hits it, the gem just reflects. But when light hits a well-cut, transparent diamond, it doesn't just reflect—it illuminates and shines.

God wants you to be as clear as a diamond and be transparent with your life. He doesn't want you to be clouded by sin. Pray to God regularly to search your heart, rummage through your thoughts, and do away with anything that isn't godly so you can live a life of radiance and brilliance.

REFLECT:

Search your heart: Is there anything that you are hiding? Is there a sin that is in your life that needs to be brought into the light?
Bring light to it, and repent to God. Pray for a clear-cut approach.

I SOCIETY

People will be lovers of themselves, lovers of money, boastful, proud, abusive,
disobedient to their parents, ungrateful, unholy, without love, unforgiving, slanderous,
without self-control, brutal, not lovers of the good, treacherous, rash, conceited,
lovers of pleasure rather than lovers of God.

—2 Timothy 3:2–4

Unfortunately, we live in a world that promotes focus on the self over others. As kids we are naturally selfish, and as we grow up we need to consciously change this behavior. You may still regularly have thoughts like *I want the front seat, I want to be first, I want attention, I want to be popular,* or *I want to sleep in and not sacrifice my time to get up early and help out.* But as long as you keep the focus on you and your gain, you won't be able to fully love God.

Selfishness pulls us away from God and draws us closer to sin, which is a reflection of your lack of fear in the Almighty God. When you don't fear God, you don't have a godly heart for others. This makes you selfish and a danger to your family, friends, and strangers. We are to live selflessly, not selfishly. Selflessness honors God.

REFLECT:

How can you live a more selfless life?
Write out 10 selfless things you could do around the house and at school.

TALK TO ME, BUDDY

I know what it's like to hold feelings inside and not talk to anyone about them. You begin to stuff the issues down deeper and continue through life as if nothing is bothering you. This works for a while, until you have stuffed down too many feelings and have no emotional real estate left—then you overflow, spewing pieces of pain out onto an innocent bystander.

This way of life is unhealthy and detrimental to your relationships with people and God. Your family and friends can sense when you're not yourself. It's better to be open and honest about your feelings with those who care about you. God wants you to know that he stands at the door patiently knocking and waiting for you to let him in. He isn't quick to speak and loose at the lips; he is a superior listener—but it's up to you to respond to his knocking. He won't force his way in, but if you let him enter, he can eradicate your hurts, sin, and pain.

REFLECT:

Are you dealing with something that you are holding in and need to talk to someone about?

I encourage you to get it off of your chest by sharing it with someone you trust and letting God in.

CONTROL FREAK

Believe it or not, a lot of people truly think that they are in charge of
their lives. I know I did for the longest time. I thought it was up to me
to make things happen. I believed that I controlled how people treated
me or how they viewed me.

I remember when I got my first car in high school and the empowering feeling of being behind the wheel. I treated life that way, too. If
something was going wrong in my family or in my life, I would try to
control the situation or fix it myself.

But living that way tends to just cause more stress and pain. God
spoke to me one day and asked, "When will you sit back and relax and
trust me to be the driver of your life?"

There are times when situations seem impossible to fix, and they
are—for you. But with God in charge, all things are possible. Leave
it to him—and stay in your lane.

REFLECT:
Are you trying to control your life right now?
*Let God make it easier for you. Stop trying to make things happen, and let
God orchestrate when and how it happens.*

Neither circumcision nor uncircumcision means anything; what counts is the new creation.
—Galatians 6:15

When you were born, you came into this world a sinner, and your life journey outside of the womb began. How do you make sure that you live a life that counts and maximize the life you were given? It starts with becoming a new creation. You should not leave here the same way you entered. You may think, is that even possible? The answer is yes. If you don't become a new creation transformed by God through making Jesus the center of your life, you will stay the exact way you came into this world, which is a sinner.

What we do here on earth is temporary when we are led by men and women. But if you allow God to lead you, you will have eternal life. When you live this way, everything counts for God. Your success should bring glory to God. Your pain and struggles should bring glory to God. Your life should be a testimony to how God has used you and should inspire others to bring glory to God through their own lives.

REFLECT:
Write out ways that you can bring glory to God through your life as a new creation.

A SPIRITUAL RELATIONSHIP

Therefore, I urge you, brothers and sisters, in view of God's mercy, to offer your bodies as a living sacrifice, holy and pleasing to God—this is your true and proper worship. Do not conform to the pattern of this world, but be transformed by the renewing of your mind. Then you will be able to test and approve what God's will is—his good, pleasing and perfect will.

—Romans 12:1-2

There is a relationship—and a distinction—between religion and spirituality. Often the two are used interchangeably in the context of faith. However, religion refers to the rituals, rules, and way to do things within a particular belief system, which may or may not be related to truly serving Jesus Christ. Spirituality, on the other hand, is simply summed up as believing. As a spiritual human being, you believe, pray, worship, read the Bible, and have a genuine relationship with Jesus Christ. It's your way of life. Christianity becomes religion when your outlook is that you "have to" versus "get to" live a life serving God.

Romans 12:1–2 is clear about what a spiritual life with God entails. "Do not conform to the pattern of this world, but be transformed by the renewing of your mind. Only then will you be able to test and approve what God's will is."

REFLECT:

You were created to have a healthy spiritual relationship with God, which includes your worship, prayers, and communication with him. Your relationship with God isn't a religion.

THE INFLUENCE OF MUSIC

Shout for joy to the Lord, all the earth, burst into jubilant song with music.
—Psalm 98:4

Music is powerful. It can evoke so many different emotions—peace, pain, joy, excitement, anger, anxiety, sadness, sensuality, intensity, and more. You know how certain songs always bring you back to a particular moment or memory? This phenomenon is similar to classical conditioning, which is associative learning, and demonstrates just how deeply music affects us.

When we sing, rap, or repeat the words of a song, they have power. They instruct and subconsciously cause us to meditate on the lyrics. Ever hear a song and catch yourself repeating it nonstop throughout the day? If you listen to it over and over, it can start to influence your views on life, your relationships, and how you respond to everyday interactions.

What you listen to can bring you either closer to or further away from God. Make sure you're feeding your spirit with lyrics that worship God and keep you in tune with the Holy Spirit. Don't take this lightly.

REFLECT:
Do you listen to a lot of worldly music?
Start listening to God-centered music from different genres, and pay attention to how it influences you.

For it is by grace you have been saved, through faith—and this is not from yourselves, it is the gift of God—not by works, so that no one can boast.

—Ephesians 2:8–9

One evening when I was in high school, my family and I went out to dinner after football practice. After my brother and I had stuffed ourselves at the buffet, my parents paid the bill, and we walked toward the car in the parking lot. My dad suddenly asked me, "Where are you going?" With a confused look on my face, I responded, "To the car." He threw a pair of keys at me and said, "Wrong car. Yours is over there." I couldn't believe it. I jumped in the air, ran to hug my parents, and thanked them profusely.

My mom and dad didn't have to buy me a car. They worked hard and wanted to bless me with a gift. And I intended to appreciate it and respect their generosity: I drove carefully, I was grateful, and I showed it.

God didn't have to send his Son to die for us and give us the chance to live eternally with him. Yet he did. When we give our life to serve him—living up to the precious gift—our sins die on that cross as well.

REFLECT:

God cares that much about you! He made a huge sacrifice to give you a gift that was unearned. God's grace is a pure gift to you. Never take it for granted.

HOW DO I GET SAVED?

If you declare with your mouth, "Jesus is Lord," and believe in your heart that God raised him from the dead, you will be saved. For it is with your heart that you believe and are justified, and it is with your mouth that you profess your faith and are saved.

—Romans 10:9–10

I once had a conversation on a high school campus with a guy who had been going to an area youth group for two years. He enjoyed the group and spoke highly of it. He asked me a question that forever changed my leadership approach. He looked me in my eye and asked, "How do I get saved?" At first I thought it was a trick question, but he was serious. From that moment on, I told myself I would never assume that everyone knows the steps to salvation.

Here is how:

1. Believe in Jesus.

2. Repent of your sins.

3. Declare with your mouth, "Jesus is Lord."

4. Fully walk away from your sinful way of life, and start the journey of walking in the faithful obedience to your Lord.

REFLECT:
Do you know anyone who might have the same question?

FAIL TO SUCCEED

Not only so, but we also glory in our sufferings, because we know that suffering produces perseverance; perseverance, character; and character, hope. And hope does not put us to shame, because God's love has been poured out into our hearts through the Holy Spirit, who has been given to us.

—Romans 5:3–5

If everything came easily, how would you grow? Sometimes we need pressure that can break us down to build us up stronger. For a muscle to grow, it has to be broken down so it can repair, replace damaged fibers, and grow back stronger. When a failure occurs, you can ask God, *What can I learn from this? How will it help me in the future?*

If you get cut from a team, are let go from a job, or fail the first semester or quarter of school, how can you learn from those situations and trust God more? These experiences are not intended to diminish you. The Bible says suffering produces perseverance—it gives you strength to endure, battle, and overcome. It fine-tunes your character and helps build your hope. God is with you in every season of your life. If you let them, your failures can be your catalyst to success.

REFLECT:
What setback are you dealing with right now?
Can you see the glory in your suffering and persevere?

DO WE EVER REALLY LOSE?

Do you not know that in a race all the runners run, but only one gets the prize? Run in such a way as to get the prize. Everyone who competes in the games goes into strict training. They do it to get a crown that will not last, but we do it to get a crown that will last forever. Therefore I do not run like someone running aimlessly; I do not fight like a boxer beating the air. No, I strike a blow to my body and make it my slave so that after I have preached to others, I myself will not be disqualified for the prize.

—1 Corinthians 9:24–27

I can't stand losing. I grew up in a competitive family, and I'll be the first to admit I didn't observe this verse from 1 Corinthians. As a teen I would never have been able to see losing (in a sports game, dance battle, video game, board game, or any competition) as ultimately winning. In my mind, you were either a winner or a loser.

And while there may be truth to that when you are competing, the mind-set shift happens after you have lost. Don't dwell on it and let it ruin your day or affect your character, because how you respond tells people about the God you serve. You never lose when you have a kingdom mind-set.

REFLECT:

You have a different motivation as a Christian. Your life demonstrates how to win daily, even if you occasionally lose. Keep God at the center of everything.

If we deliberately keep on sinning after we have received the knowledge of the truth, no sacrifice for sins is left.

—Hebrews 10:26

Why do I keep doing the same thing over and over again? I know that it is wrong and I should not be engaging in this action, but I can't stop. I try to stop—I can go a few days and not do it, but then I slip up and have to start over again. Trying to overcome addiction by yourself is extremely tough to do. Remember that you are not alone. There are many multistep programs out there to help treat addiction. However, if you remove or don't add Jesus's healing power into the mix, it's truly hard to overcome.

God wants you to overcome addicting sin. First you have to identify that you are in fact addicted. If you can't stop and you deliberately keep on sinning after knowing that it is sin, you are in a dangerous place of rejecting Christ. Addiction is real, and you need accountability alongside Jesus in the process of beating it. Have someone check up on you. Distance yourself from what tempts you.

Spend time praying, reading, and worshipping God. Jesus himself suffered when he was tempted; he is able to help those who are being tempted. He will set you free.

REFLECT:
If you are addicted to something in your life, don't hide it. You can get help by reaching out to your youth pastor, your school guidance counselor, or the American Addiction Centers (1-888-726-1868).
Take it day by day, one step at a time, and celebrate your wins.

TREAT PEOPLE HOW YOU WANT TO BE TREATED

"So in everything, do to others what you would have them do to you,
for this sums up the Law and the Prophets."
—Matthew 7:12

We hear this piece of Scripture so much that it sometimes loses its impact. If you hear or see something often enough, you can become desensitized to it. But there's a reason it is repeated so often.

The greatest decision you will ever make is choosing to follow Jesus Christ, but it won't make life easier all of a sudden. Choosing to be a Christian requires you to live life the way it is taught in the Bible.

A serious change of heart takes place through the process of living God's way. You are young and still learning who you are, and it's not always easy to figure out how to live a life that is pleasing to God. This is a great verse to inform you on how to be a disciple of Christ. In everything, treat others the way you would have them treat you. It is direct and simple, and it gives you an awareness of God's heart. It also brings attention to your actions toward others.

So don't make fun of someone if you don't want to be made fun of; don't bully someone if you don't want to be bullied. Don't try to manipulate people to get what you want if you don't want the same thing done to you. It's truly that simple.

REFLECT:
Do you treat the people around you the way you want to be treated? Write out ways you can be better at this.

INCLUDE GOD IN EVERY DECISION

I will instruct you and teach you in the way you should go;
I will counsel you with my loving eye on you.

—Psalm 32:8

During my senior year of high school, I felt as if life suddenly became more adult. I had a lot of decisions I had to make regarding my future, and it was overwhelming. I knew I was going to receive a football scholarship, but I didn't know where I would choose to spend the next four years of my life. Should I go across the country or stay close to home?

I knew that there was wisdom in counsel. I sat down with wise people I trusted; they were Christians, so I knew they had my best interests in mind. My parents came with me on college visits. I prayed to God before bed every night for him to direct me. This helped me keep God in the loop and comforted me through my decision-making process.

I encourage you to involve God in all your decisions, big and small—including which parties to go to, classes to take, colleges to choose, and friends to have around. God will never steer you astray. He loves you unlike anyone you know.

REFLECT:
What decisions do you have to make?
Write them down, and pray over them every night before bed.
God will direct you.

TELL THE TRUTH

Whoever conceals their sins does not prosper, but the one who confesses
and renounces them finds mercy.

—Proverbs 28:13

You are better off just telling the truth. The trauma of telling the truth pales in comparison to the task of trying to keep the truth hidden and having to lie about it consistently.

I've been on both sides of this. Lying doesn't feel any better, and there is no freedom in it. It may take people a while to accept the truth, but in the end they will always respect you for it. You need to consciously think about telling the truth in all situations. If you don't, you will catch yourself lying to your parents or peers about the silliest things, which will hurt you in the long run because they won't be able to trust you.

Scripture says, "Whoever conceals their sins does not prosper, but the one who confesses and renounces them finds mercy." If you can't be trusted by your friends, teachers, parents, coworkers, or siblings, that perception of untrustworthiness can hinder you from prospering and being successful. The truth gives you freedom and sets you free of the enemy's traps.

REFLECT:
Are there any lies for which you need to ask God for forgiveness and repent?
Be more mindful with your actions so that you don't put yourself in a scenario where you feel the need to lie. Obey your parents, and save yourself the temptation of lying.

LIFE WITH A SINGLE PARENT

He heals the brokenhearted and binds up their wounds.
—Psalm 147:3

Fewer than half (46 percent) of US kids younger than 18 years of age are living in homes with two married parents in their first marriage. If you have a single parent at home, know that you are not alone. Chances are there are lots of guys at your school going through the same thing.

You may be happy that your parents split because they aren't fighting any longer. Or maybe for you, it's devastating and feels unfair. Either way, a single-parent household comes with its unique challenges and circumstances. You don't have to be bitter or afraid of commitment, act out, or seek validation from your peers. Appreciate the great attributes your parent displays, admire their strength to do it on their own, and recognize the amazing sacrifices they make for you every day.

God wants you to know he is there to heal your broken heart and repair your wounds. It's okay to display sadness, pain, and anger sometimes—it's only natural. But lean on God's love and wisdom to guide you.

REFLECT:
Are you dealing with challenging emotions from a living in a single-parent home?
Talk to someone. You are not alone.

STRENGTH THROUGH PAIN

"Then I would still have this consolation—my joy in unrelenting pain—
that I had not denied the words of the Holy One."

—Job 6:10

It's easy to say you believe in Jesus Christ when everything is going well and you experience earthly blessings in your life. But even more important is how you respond to Jesus when injury, pain, or confusion finds its way into your life. No doubt about it, you will experience setbacks along your journey. During those setbacks, God will test your faith, your friendships, and your inner strength.

There's a guy in the Bible named Job who went through the ultimate test of his strength and faith. He lost a lot in his life, but he took pride in knowing that through his pain he would never deny God. When tough times strike, you have an opportunity to show people how amazing God is through pain and struggle. You can be the symbol of peace in devastation and tap in to a strength that you didn't know you had. There is a blessing in your pain. Trust that God is taking you to a new level.

REFLECT:

Are you dealing with an injury, illness, or setback right now?
Read the story of Job and what he went through. Use his story to give you hope and strength.

GOD IS YOUR CONSTANT

Why, my soul, are you downcast? Why so disturbed within me?
Put your hope in God, for I will yet praise him, my Savior and my God.
—Psalm 42:11

He was the new kid in town. All the guys wanted to be around him, the girls thought he was cute, his home life was great, and he was strong and athletic. He had a great youth group he attended every week. His Bible study group also met every week. He had leaders who took an interest in him and made sure he was doing okay.

Then life got tougher for him. He didn't really know how to handle his emotions and actions. He stopped going to Bible study, responding to leaders, and attending youth group. The pressures of school and life made him want to be alone. He pushed people away and then felt like they had turned their backs on him. But that was exactly what the enemy wanted. The devil tries to create loneliness and confusion.

Sometimes you may feel like people let you down, but remember they are not perfect. Only God can be your perfect constant. Put your hope in God to carry you when no one else is there for you.

REFLECT:

Do you struggle with loneliness?
Do you feel like others have let you down or abandoned you?
Put your faith in God. Ask him to help you get connected again.
Know that no one is like our God. He is perfect, and people aren't.

HE WILL HEAR YOU

"If my people, who are called by my name, will humble themselves and pray and seek my face and turn from their wicked ways, then I will hear from Heaven, and I will forgive their sin and will heal their land."

—2 Chronicles 7:14

Do you find yourself confused about how to actually talk to God? You hear your pastors or seasoned Christians pray with such eloquence; maybe it intimidates you because you don't understand how they can string words and Scriptures together to sound so holy. The truth is that you can talk to God with any kind of vernacular. God wants to hear from you.

Be sure to be genuine when you open your mouth to talk to God. Give him thanks for allowing you to breathe, giving you a roof over your head, blessing you with a brain to reason, and giving you an opportunity to live in eternity. Truly think about what you say because specific prayers get specific answers from God. Talk to him as you would talk to your friends. Read your Bible, and let the Scriptures bring life to your prayers.

Prayer is a simple step for the ordinary that yields extraordinary results.

REFLECT:
Try praying in your own voice today, and don't compare yourself to anyone else.

LOOK IN THE MIRROR

But in your hearts revere Christ as Lord. Always be prepared to give an answer to everyone who asks you to give the reason for the hope that you have. But do this with gentleness and respect.

—1 Peter 3:15

There will be people who won't understand your choice to live a life that follows the Word of God. But people often make fun of things they don't understand. Every day you have an opportunity to represent the love of Jesus Christ, and most of the time your actions make more of an impact than what you say.

You must give others respect—even those who disagree with you—while always honoring, revering, and respecting Jesus Christ with all of your heart. You will be questioned about your faith, the way you carry yourself, and your choice to live for God. Some people will try to rattle you so that you lose your cool. First Peter 3:15 reminds you to always respond "with gentleness and respect." You will model Jesus Christ by not responding negatively.

REFLECT:
How can you model Jesus and respect him at all times, even when your faith is questioned?
Always cling to humility and take the higher path.

YOU CAN'T GET SLEEP BACK

In peace I will lie down and sleep, for you alone, LORD,
make me dwell in safety.

—Psalm 4:8

Have you ever had trouble sleeping because something's weighing on your mind? *Will those guys bully me again tomorrow? Am I ready for that big test in two days? I'm so excited for the big game this week. I just don't feel like sleeping—I like staying up late.*

I know the world we live in tells us that you can sleep when you're dead, that you need to hustle and grind 24/7. But the truth is, you can never get back those lost hours of sleep, and lying wide awake thinking about your anxieties will only hurt your performance the next day.

There will be issues and obstacles that you will not be able to control. God wants you to have peace in knowing that he is working on your behalf while you get your much-needed rest. You need sleep to be the best that God has called you to be.

REFLECT:
What are you losing sleep over?
Trust that God will help you through it and help you get your sleep.

EMOTIONS ON THE RUN

Like a city whose walls are broken through is a person who lacks self-control.
—Proverbs 25:28

I had a bad day and didn't want to be around anyone. Of course, that day my brother chose to test me. Younger siblings love to push you to the limits at the wrong time. I told my brother, "Not today. Leave me alone." He kept bothering me as I tried to watch TV and brood. I finally put my foot down and asked him, "Do you want to fight?" I was at my tipping point and couldn't control my emotions any longer. I started walking toward him, seeing red, until my dad intercepted the wrath that was coming my brother's way.

I didn't want to hurt my dad, so I darted past him, ran into the bathroom, and, totally lacking in self-control, exploded. I broke almost everything in the bathroom as I acted on my rage. My unhappiness and pain had built up inside of me and caused me to act unlike myself.

The enemy wants us to act without control over our emotions. Lack of control could wreck our lives—one bad decision could alter the course of our lives forever. With God's wisdom we learn how to operate with control and not let our emotions rule and ruin us. I was lucky it was just a few bathroom accessories that I trashed; as I cleaned up the mess, I prayed for self-control and responsibility over my temper.

REFLECT:
Do you struggle with keeping your emotions in check? Take time to meditate and pray daily. Start with just five minutes a day and build up from there.

BEAUTIFUL POVERTY

The LORD sends poverty and wealth; he humbles and he exalts.

—1 Samuel 2:7

It doesn't feel fair that my mother has to work three jobs just to keep a roof over our heads and food on our table. Why would God allow us to be in this situation? I can't go to school without people making fun of the holes in my shoes.

God doesn't want you to be poor; he works in your best interest for everlasting life. The Bible mentions that it's hard for a rich person to enter into Heaven because he feels as if he doesn't need God, because he has wealth. Both wealthy and poor people have their problems. When you are able to rely more on God than wealth, it becomes a true blessing.

Hard times can give you strength to persevere. A strong relationship with God during the toughest times of your life will benefit you when the blessings come. Rather than sulking at your current status, praise God for his saving grace to make sure you will live eternally and not just for the material world.

REFLECT:

Are you living in a financially tough situation? Write about it. Pray that God will show you the blessing in this rubble and that you will never lose sight of him when he exalts you out of the ashes.

KEEP YOUR HANDS OFF

It is God's will that you should be sanctified: that you should avoid sexual immorality;
that each of you should learn to control your own body in a way that is holy and honorable,
not in passionate lust like the pagans, who do not know God.

—1 Thessalonians 4:3–5

The Bible tells us to avoid sexual immorality and have self-control over our bodies in a way that is holy and honorable. Your purity is compromised when you give in to the sin of lust. When you fantasize and have lustful thoughts, it becomes sin. Not too many guys have nice, pure thoughts while they engage in sexual acts.

You need to ask yourself why you want to commit sin. What types of thoughts or external influences are compromising your mind? Masturbation can become an addicting act—it puts you in a bad position in which you will continue to knowingly sin and thereby create a gap between you and God.

If your internal influence is pure, absent of lust and sexual thoughts, you'll avoid sin.

REFLECT:

If you struggle in this department, know that you are not alone. Reach out to an authoritative figure to hold you accountable and actively pay attention to what you look at, listen to, and read. Guard yourself.

DON'T CAUSE CONFLICT

A troublemaker and a villain, who goes about with a corrupt mouth, who winks maliciously with his eye, signals with his feet and motions with his fingers, who plots evil with deceit in his heart—he always stirs up conflict. Therefore disaster will overtake him in an instant; he will suddenly be destroyed—without remedy.

—Proverbs 6:12–15

We all know the troublemakers who like to stir up conflict in any setting that they can, just to get a rise out of people. Occasionally pulling pranks or cracking jokes with each other is harmless and fun among friends.

But troublemakers do more than just prank—they try to spark an emotional response in a negative way. It becomes serious when a person has corruption in their heart and plots to say and do inflammatory things to hurt people or evoke arguments.

I want you to know that God hates a person who stirs up conflict in any community. Proverbs 6:12–15 shows us that God means business about his disgust with these actions.

Stay away from troublemakers. Do not respond to them or get caught in their web of evil.

REFLECT:

Do you like to start trouble? Know that God takes these actions seriously. Work on changing how you treat people. Ask for their forgiveness and repent to God.

CAN I HEAR FROM GOD?

"Call to me and I will answer you and tell you great and unsearchable things you do not know."
—Jeremiah 33:3

I guarantee that if you were in a large crowded setting, like the mall or a sports event, and your mom or dad started yelling your name, for some reason you would hear their voice and know who was calling you. Why? It's because you know your parents intimately—especially their voices. It's the same thing with being able to hear God. He is speaking to you all the time. The question is, are you tuned in to hear his voice?

If you really want to hear from God, you have desire to and believe you will hear from him. God's communication style isn't like the way we communicate with each other. It's a very subtle prompting in your spirit that you can hear in your mind, as if it's a whisper. That whisper becomes clearer and stronger the closer you are to God. It takes a consistent relationship with him to gain confidence in his voice.

God wants you to call on him regularly. He wants to communicate and answer you. His voice will never go against his word in the Bible, so if you ever feel confused about his message, check the Bible for confirmation.

REFLECT:
Always ask God to give you a Scripture on a decision in your life. Call on God regularly, and tune in to his voice.

FOCUS ON YOUR ABILITIES

The Lord is good to all; he has compassion on all he has made.
—Psalm 145:9

Compared to God, we have such limited minds. You may see a bossy student, and God sees the next president. You may see a class clown who can be annoying at times, and God sees the next comedian who helps heal hearts through laughter. You may see a studious nerd with no friends, and God sees the next neurologist making a breakthrough to cure disease. You may see a disability in a person, but God sees a beautiful human being with unique, unmatched gifts. You may only see negative things when you look at yourself, too.

Instead of focusing on your or someone else's perceived shortcomings, focus on their God-given abilities. We are to treat everyone how God treats us. The Bible says that the Lord is good to all and that he has compassion for all he has made. You may feel as though you are not gifted or special, but let me remind you that you are created in the image of God. You are placed here with a purpose, which means you have an amazing natural ability.

REFLECT:

Ask God to reveal and highlight your abilities. We all have our insecurities that we battle. Don't let those overshadow the abilities God gave you. See the unique abilities in others.

I WANT TO BELIEVE

Doubt is to call into question the truth of something. It is a normal response that we must embrace and challenge daily. If you are uncertain about something, it's okay to inquire about it. Students ask me all the time about God: How do I know that he is real?

I'll share a story from when I was about three years old. My mother was hit by a car, and it rolled over her. I saw her lose consciousness and slip away for over 30 seconds. Then, from the back of a police car, I watched the paramedics revive her.

Doctors said that she would never walk again. Today, through God's miraculous hand, she is walking fine, and she is a pastor alongside my dad, helping so many people. This experience plagued me throughout my life—I was at once angry and happy with God. *Thank you, thank you for saving my mother*. And yet, why would he allow this to happen? Nine years later, I made a choice to believe that God was at work in this accident and to live for him and not doubt him. Doubt will leave you unstable and unhappy. Choose to observe the miracles of God's work all around you. Do not give in to doubt.

REFLECT:

Are you having trouble fully believing in and not doubting God?
If so, talk to someone about it. Give God a chance to radically change
your life. You have to wholeheartedly believe and not waver back
and forth.

FRENEMIES

There will be moments in your life when you can't believe the actions of a friend, peer, coworker, parent, teacher, or pastor. When you are close with others, you become vulnerable with them and share a lot about your life. They see your faults, and you recognize their limitations. Not every friend you have will be who they say they are. People change, and if you don't change with them, a natural divide may occur.

Life happens in seasons. In certain seasons of life, your friendships may require deeper connections; other seasons may lead to distance between you. I've lost friends in the past who turned on me or openly persecuted me. The worst was hearing about how they spoke behind my back and then watching them pretend everything was fine when they saw me in person.

God wants you to bless them regardless and not retaliate against or curse them. Trust God, and watch him work it out for good.

REFLECT:
Write out a list of how you can respond in a godly way versus your gut reaction. This will give you an advantage when you find yourself in a tricky situation.

NO FILTER NEEDED

After all, no one ever hated their own body, but they feed and care for their body, just as Christ does the church.

—Ephesians 5:29

Almost every professional picture you see posted on a billboard, in a magazine, in online campaigns, on social media, and in commercials is altered. Imperfections are smoothed away, filters are applied, and lighting is used to highlight all the best features. We see this so much that subconsciously we begin to believe that these images are real and that we have to look a particular way—whether it's our bodies, hairstyles, clothes, skin, or any number of other elements.

This has serious consequences. When measured up against these unrealistic standards, it's easy to believe you are not good enough. This starts to influence how you view yourself. You may be compelled to apply a metaphorical filter to yourself, just so that you can fit in and gain approval. All the while, God wants you to love yourself the way you are. After all, it's not natural to hate yourself. You were not created to despise yourself but to care for the person God lovingly made.

Don't let outside influences lie to you and tell you that you are not good enough. You need no filter. You're perfect as you are.

REFLECT:

Do you feel like you aren't good enough at times? Remember that you are meant to love yourself and who God has made you to be. Don't change for anybody. Be yourself!

FIND BALANCE IN YOUR EATING

"The thief comes only to steal and kill and destroy;
I have come that they may have life, and have it to the full."
—John 10:10

I knew a kid who was made fun of for being overweight. He had a bad relationship with food and couldn't find the balance between eating enough and overeating. He knew only one speed, and that was to eat as much as possible as quickly as he could. His life consisted of eating, going to school, doing homework, watching television, and playing video games.

The name-calling and teasing started to wear on him when his eyes caught sight of a young lady at school and he developed an interest in her. This girl was athletic, beautiful, funny, and well liked. He didn't think he had a chance with her, so he began to take drastic measures to change himself and starved his body. When he did eat, he would make himself throw up in the bathroom. One day in PE class, the young man passed out from dehydration and was rushed to the hospital. If he hadn't passed out that day, something more tragic could have happened.

There are better ways to be healthy. God wants you to have a full life, and the enemy wants to rob you of it. Please don't allow others to dictate your eating habits and health. Every body is different. Make changes in a healthful way. Never assume you know the experiences of others.

REFLECT:
If you are dealing with an eating disorder, please don't shoulder it alone. Reach out to your parents, an authority figure, or the National Eating Disorders Association helpline at 1-800-931-2237.

YOU CAN'T SERVE TWO MASTERS

"No one can serve two masters. Either you will hate the one and love the other, or you will be devoted to the one and despise the other. You cannot serve both God and money."
—Matthew 6:24

As a young man, I was encouraged to enjoy different hobbies such as sketching, reading, video games, and playing sports. I would do those things nonstop. Every day I found a way to participate in each of these hobbies, and I loved them. The reading and drawing gave me a sense of stillness, peace, and creativity. Video games were a fun way to get lost in a different world. But it was sports that seemed to consume every area of my life. I would participate in, read about, sketch, and watch sports constantly.

You may have noticed that I didn't mention how much time I spent with God and getting to know him consistently. That's because I didn't make time for God consistently outside of our family going to church and occasionally reading my Bible. That is backward living. The Bible says no one can serve two masters: We can't love the things of this temporal world and love God at the same time. You can enjoy the things of this world, but they can't take the place of the true master. God comes first, and we are to serve only him.

REFLECT:
Are you trying to serve two masters?
Evaluate your current hobbies and interests, and make sure they don't take the place of God's true position in your life.

CHOOSE CAREFULLY

Be very careful, then, how you live—not as unwise but as wise, making the most of every opportunity, because the days are evil. Therefore do not be foolish, but understand what the Lord's will is.

—Ephesians 5:15–17

There is nothing wrong with going to parties when you choose carefully. You don't need to go to every party you're invited to. The beautiful thing about being connected to God on a daily basis is the prompting of wisdom you get from the Holy Spirit.

You have to consider who is throwing the party, what type of people will be there, and if it's wise for you to be in attendance. A girl in our youth group was told by her parents not to go to a friend's party because they didn't feel good about it. Both of her parents are pastors and have strong power of discernment. She disobeyed her parents that night and went to the party. She left at the end of the party with people she thought were friends, but she never made it back home.

Her loss was devastating and a powerful lesson to be careful about your choices and who you align yourself with. The devil prowls around seeking to devour. When those who are wiser than you speak, trust them.

REFLECT:
Don't be afraid to pray about all the decisions you must make in your life. You are in good hands when you involve God in your everyday judgment. Trust the wisdom of your parents and other authorities.

BUT WHERE'S MY SOUL MATE?

So the LORD God caused the man to fall into a deep sleep; and while he was sleeping, he took one of the man's ribs and then closed up the place with flesh. Then the LORD God made a woman from the rib he had taken out of the man, and he brought her to the man. The man said, "This is now bone of my bones and flesh of my flesh; she shall be called 'woman,' for she was taken out of man." That is why a man leaves his father and mother and is united to his wife, and they become one flesh.

—Genesis 2:21–24

The term *soul mate* is thrown around a lot in society. Your peers may say they can't wait to find their soul mates or that they think they have already. But the concept of a soul mate isn't biblical and isn't real. The Bible doesn't tell you that there is one specific person for you. As a Christian, you are not infallible, and you can marry the wrong person. If you choose to be with a nonbeliever, it will make you "unequally yoked" (2 Corinthians 6:14), which means you won't be able to work together as a productive team in your marriage. You are able to marry someone of the same faith, which will make you equally yoked. This will help alleviate a lot of problems and create a harmonious future in your marriage.

Whomever you choose to marry one day will be the one for you because she will share your faith, and you will become one.

REFLECT:

Don't be in a rush to find your wife. Get to know God and yourself first. When you spend time getting to know God, you get to know yourself better and can make better godly decisions. That will put you in a better position to choose a godly wife someday.

Whoever walks in integrity walks securely, but whoever takes crooked paths will be found out.
—Proverbs 10:9

Think twice about putting off your homework and not paying attention in class. Cramming the day of your test and then sitting next to the smart person to sneak a peek at their answers isn't the route you should take. That is taking the easy way out and what the Bible would call the crooked path.

You are setting the tone of your life. Cheating isn't honest. The Bible says whoever walks in integrity walks confidently. There isn't a better feeling than knowing you took your test and did well because you put in hard work.

Unfortunately, you often hear about athletes and politicians acting without integrity and cheating. Cheating can be taking steroids or manipulating something for the outcome you want. The temptation to cheat will always be there, but it's not worth the sacrifice of your integrity. The habits you form now will shape the man you will become in the future.

REFLECT:
When the temptation to cheat comes knocking on your door, don't answer it. Think about the value of your integrity and don't waver.

I know your deeds, your hard work and your perseverance.
—Revelation 2:2

How can you be a great student? First things first, you have to change any negative perspective about school. It has to change from disdain to excitement. You won't like every aspect of school—no one expects that—but you should try to enjoy it and see the value of it. Right now, school is your job.

As a student, your job is to attend school on time, learn, do well, and graduate. School takes hard work when you do it right, and it pays off beautifully in the long run when you do it unto the Lord. If you are blessed to not have to work on top of attending school, be grateful. If you have a job outside of school to earn money, remember that both of these jobs are equally important.

Revelation 2:2 reminds us that working God knows how hard we work. Strive to be the best student you can be, and in the end you will learn how to be the greatest worker you can be, which is pleasing to the Lord.

REFLECT:
Ask yourself, Do I work hard as a student?
Do you take this "job" seriously?
Make the commitment to prioritize your life in this order:
   1. God
   2. Family
   3. School

GOSSIP GUY

A gossip betrays a confidence; so avoid anyone who talks too much.
—Proverbs 20:19

Isn't it great to get the scoop on what's going on in the entertainment and sports worlds? You love hearing about the recent drama of your favorite celebrity or superstar athlete. You don't truly know if the news is accurate, of course. As a society we take media gossip and gobble it up, rarely taking the time to find out if it's factual or not.

When you spread secrets, either true or false, you become a gossiper. Once you are labeled a gossiper, it's hard for people to trust you. Friends, family, or acquaintances will watch what they say around you. If someone shared confidential information with you, it's because they trusted that you could keep information to yourself. A gossiper lacks self-control.

The Bible says to avoid anyone who talks too much, because a two-faced person is a dangerous person. Be careful of those who speak in excessive flattery; often this is to gain favor with you and get information out of you. Gossiping doesn't help anyone; it tears down relationships and people. We are not to engage in gossip.

REFLECT:

Pay attention to the conversations you enter, and try to identify if they are fruitful conversation or gossip. If someone confides in you, keep the information to yourself.

UPLIFTING SPEECH

The words of the reckless pierce like swords, but the tongue of the wise brings healing.
—Proverbs 12:18

Ask yourself, "What type of person do I want to be?" Do you want to be one who is always negative, quick to say no, and sees something wrong in everything? Or would you like to be the person who brings positive thoughts and energy?

No one is perfect, and no one can be in a great mood every day, but we can control what we say. Some people take pride in having a quick tongue, ready to tear someone down with a cutting response. Sometimes you may not even realize how much you criticize others.

Without thought, the outcome can be reckless speech. Out of the heart, the mouth speaks. Our negativity is a direct reflection of our heart.

Pray on this, and give yourself a chance to uproot the weeds of negativity and plant new seeds of life-giving positivity. The tongue of the wise brings healing and benefits to those they encounter. These actions illustrate a healthy spirit and mind led by our God of wisdom.

REFLECT:
Crave to be one who is slow to criticize, quick to listen, and excited to lift up others.

TRUE HAPPINESS

Taste and see that the LORD is good; blessed is the one who takes refuge in him.
—Psalm 34:8

Throughout most of high school, I appeared happy and excited about life. I had parents who loved each other and loved my brother and me deeply. I had a house with a roof over my head, clothes on my back, shoes on my feet, and food on the table. I was blessed to have God-given athletic ability, which opened doors for me. I got along with a lot of my peers. The creative in me had an outlet in art and poetry to release stress. You would think that happiness was my middle name.

But earthly happiness fulfills only the flesh; it's extremely shallow and doesn't have depth. When I was made fun of because of my complexion, where I lived, and who I was trying to be, it was painful. I didn't understand why God wouldn't just make me like everybody else.

I was missing true happiness because I didn't make God my source of joy. If we try to get our validation from our peers, it sets us up for failure. It wasn't until I tried and experienced the Lord for myself that I was able to find true happiness—during the good times, in confusion, and in the middle of a storm.

REFLECT:
Step up to the challenge, and don't wait until you get older to find your joy, hope, and true happiness in the Lord. You can save yourself from plenty of heartache if you tap in to God now.

PAIN IS NOT YOUR PENALTY

And the God of all grace, who called you to his eternal glory in Christ, after you have suffered a little while, will himself restore you and make you strong, firm and steadfast.

—1 Peter 5:10

You have the free will to make decisions in life. Who will be your tour guide? Will you let the enemy fool you into thinking that your pain means you can take control of your life—when truly he is steering the rudder of your boat? Or will you let the author and finisher of your faith lead you in love and know that every season in your life has a purpose?

Those moments filled with pain, rage, discouragement, shame, and unworthiness knit you into the creation that God is perfecting. You are not perfect, but you are perfect for him to use, to bring glory to his name and shed light on the redeeming grace of God. Though you may suffer, God will restore you and make you strong. Sometimes the hurricanes you face are not meant to cause damage to your life; some are there to clear the debris so that you can walk a path that's devoid of strife.

REFLECT:

What pain are you dealing with?
Take it to God, and speak freely to him. Ask for mentors, leaders, and the right friends to come along and be your strength and support network to lean on during these tough times. Have the confidence to know that God is with you every step of the way.

THE FUTURE YOU

Listen to advice and accept discipline, and at the end you will be counted among the wise. Many are the plans in a person's heart, but it is the Lord's purpose that prevails.

—Proverbs 19:20–21

I know it feels as if you are told what to do all the time. During these years of your life, there is a maturation that needs to take place, and you need the proper guidance to set you up for success. Time goes by fast—in the blink of an eye you will be moving on to your next phase of life.

The Bible tells you to accept that you have not had a lot of life experience, and the Lord wants to prepare you for the life that is before you. The storybook of your life has been written. Be willing to be taught, refined, advised, and directed so that one day you will be a man of wisdom guided by the Lord.

Don't let your youth rob you of the life God intends for you to live here on earth. The future you will thank you.

REFLECT:
When you receive wisdom, guidance, or instruction, take it to heart. Thank God for his care over your life.

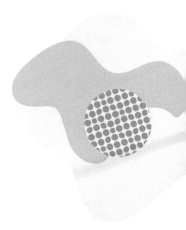

YOU NEVER KNOW

Do everything without grumbling or arguing, so that you may become blameless and pure,
"children of God without fault in a warped and crooked generation."
Then you will shine among them like stars in the sky.
—Philippians 2:14–15

One Saturday morning my dad woke my brother and me up extra early and told us to get dressed and ready for the day. Waking up early on a Saturday morning was not cool. We were accustomed to sleeping in, waking up to Mom's pancakes, lounging, watching television or playing video games, and then going outside to play all day. This particular morning, I'll admit, I had a bad attitude.

I got dressed, grumbling the whole time. My dad said, "Stop complaining. Stick with me, and big things will happen." He would always say that. Normally I would get excited, but that day I wasn't having it. We hopped in the car and took off, and I could feel myself dozing off in the passenger seat. I woke up in the parking lot of the Ohio State football stadium. We were at an Ohio State vs. Washington football game, with my favorite player, Eddie George, playing. My dad was so gracious, but I had to apologize for my grumbling. Like the great father he is, he was so excited to bless us with this gift that he forgave me.

When I look back, I regret the time I wasted on petty complaints. I missed out on the anticipation—and I almost talked myself out of a wonderful gift.

REFLECT:
God wants to set you apart from your generation of complainers.
Hold your attitude and tongue captive, argue and complain less,
and watch how you will shine like a diamond in dirt.

YOU ARE ADOPTED

And, "I will be a Father to you, and you will be my sons and daughters,
says the Lord Almighty."
—2 Corinthians 6:18

A father plays a significant role in a son's life. He helps shape the type of man that you will become. Dads can boost a son's confidence and self-esteem just by being present in their lives. A dad can play a major role in helping you develop great social skills and minimize bad relationships. Your dad can shape your belief system and your spiritual walk and guide you along your journey of manhood.

Well, I wish this applied to me, you might be thinking. I can understand if you feel like you don't have an earthly father. Maybe your dad left when you were young, departed this earth too soon, or just isn't a strong presence in your life. I'm so sorry for your loss. And I want you to know that God wants to be a father to you. His arms are open wide and his heart is full of love for you. He wants to guide and show you the way and be the father your earthly father can't be.

REFLECT:

If you are struggling with a relationship with your earthly father, reach out to him and try to talk about it.
I want you to take some time in prayer and picture God saying 2 Corinthians 6:18 over you. Accept his words.

TREAT WOMEN WITH RESPECT

Treat younger men as brothers, older women as mothers,
and younger women as sisters, with absolute purity.

—1 Timothy 5:2

Your mother is a special, beautiful, uniquely powerful woman created by God. Do you realize the strength it took to bring you into this world? You are one of your mom's greatest achievements. You are not always going to agree with your mom; that's only natural. But remember that you must always respect women. Your sister will drive you crazy, girls at school may annoy you, and some teachers may bore you, but they are all deserving of respect.

The Bible tells you to treat women with respect—to treat older women as mothers and younger women as sisters, with absolute purity. This means that you should also show respect to women by not lusting after them.

Of course, you will find some women attractive, but that doesn't give you the license to cross boundaries just because you feel like it. Control your anger and desire, and bridle your tongue when it comes to women. Remove yourself from the presence of guys who choose to disrespect women and women who don't respect themselves.

REFLECT:
How can you motivate other guys to respect girls and women through your words and actions?
You guys are leaders. Remember that!

Jesus said, "Father, forgive them, for they do not know what they are doing."
And they divided up his clothes by casting lots.

—Luke 23:34

Jesus was humiliated, mocked, spit on, beaten, and hung on a cross in the most heartbreaking and painful way. While he was hanging there, the criminals crucified next to him criticized and insulted him. Jesus could look down and see people disrespecting him and gambling for his clothes. On top of the physical pain he had to endure, he also had to deal with embarrassment and mental anguish.

One of the things that Jesus couldn't stop thinking about was forgiveness. His prayer was, "Father, forgive them, for they do not know what they are doing." I don't know about you, but that would not have been my thought process. I would have said, "God, I'm tired of this. I'm getting down, healing myself, and beating everyone down there with this cross." Thank goodness for everyone that Jesus wasn't like that.

You will encounter embarrassment and humiliation from peers, family, coaches, teachers, and even strangers online, but it's not your place to withhold forgiveness. You are not their judge. God forgives us daily for our sins. We must offer the same response, even in times of humiliation.

REFLECT:
Have you been humiliated and embarrassed and not forgiven people for it? Whom do you need to forgive today?

ADMIRE THEIR CREATOR

Peter and the other apostles replied: "We must obey God rather than human beings!"
—Acts 5:29

We all have someone we admire. Most of the time, we're drawn to a gift or talent they have. You may look up to a musician, actor, athlete, teacher, pastor, or peer. It's always great to admire or appreciate someone else; it can inspire and motivate you to be better. It may even spark a desire inside you to do what they are doing, not realizing that God used them to bring that gift out of you.

But sometimes we begin to admire a person more than the Creator of that person, which can become a problem. We are to bring attention and glory to God, who created all of our gifts. People have prominent positions in our lives, but God should hold the top spot.

God uses people in our lives to impact and direct us, but he will never replace himself in your life with a human being. God comes first in everything.

REFLECT:

Whom do you admire? What do you admire about them? Give God thanks for the gifts he instills in you and others.

DO NOT BE FRIGHTENED

But even if you should suffer for what is right, you are blessed.
"Do not fear their threats; do not be frightened."

—1 Peter 3:14

His dad would come home late at night completely drunk. Instead of coming home to his wife and kids after work, he would stop by the nearest bar with his buddies or sometimes by himself and consume too much. When he would come home, he would yell at his kids and occasionally verbally and physically abuse his wife. The family suffered and didn't know what to do. The son suffered internally because there were moments when his dad was amazing and loving. But when he would take out his anger on the family, it would hurt him. He was torn because he just wanted a dad to look up to, love, and be loved by.

First Peter 3:14 says that if you should suffer for what is right, you will be blessed. Do not be frightened. After praying on this Scripture, the young man did just that. He went to his youth pastor, finally shared what was going on at home, and asked for help. This took humility and strength, which became catalysts for change. His mother agreed to meet and get help from leaders at the church. Then his father agreed as well. Now they are headed in the right direction for healing in their family.

REFLECT:
Are you in a place where you are scared to stand up for what's right? If so, write what that is, and take it to God. He wants to help and bless you.

GLOW IN THE DARK

"You are the light of the world. A town built on a hill cannot be hidden. Neither do people light a lamp and put it under a bowl. Instead they put it on its stand, and it gives light to everyone in the house. In the same way, let your light shine before others, that they may see your good deeds and glorify your Father in Heaven."

—Matthew 5:14–16

It was a beautiful evening, and my wife was out of town. I set up an indoor camping scenario for my two daughters. I opened a tent in our living room in front of the TV. We ate dinner and watched a movie under glow-in-the-dark stars.

The dark living room represents the world that we live in. When we know and follow Jesus, we are called to be a light in this world. We are not to dim our light to try to fit in; we need to stay lit in order to pierce through the darkness. At the end of the movie that night with my girls, they noticed that the glow-in-the-dark stars were not as bright. My oldest asked me, "Daddy, what happened to the stars?" I explained that in order for the stars to shine bright, they first need to be exposed to a bright source of light.

As do we. We need to stay connected to Jesus on a daily basis in order to keep our light bright.

REFLECT:

Write a list of ways you can stay connected to Jesus daily.
What do you do to spread your light and allow others to see it? Imagine your actions and smile being so bright and radiant that they catch the attention of all your peers.

Trust in the Lord with all your heart and lean not on your own understanding;
in all your ways submit to him, and he will make your paths straight

—Proverbs 3:5–6

Most of the time we think having control of a situation guarantees the outcome we want. But trying to control the world will backfire.

In middle school, my friend wanted a girlfriend because he thought having a girlfriend would help him fit in with his boys. He took control of the situation and asked a girl to be his girlfriend. She said yes, and he was excited for a few weeks—until his boys started making fun of him and complaining about how they never saw him anymore. This was not what he had envisioned, and he ended up breaking her heart. If he had left it up to God, he would have realized it wasn't the right season to have a girlfriend and would have spared the feelings of this young girl.

The need to control can do serious damage to others. The people we try to control end up feeling as if they are not good enough. And the things that we are trying to avoid by taking control—failure, criticism, disappointment, depression, rejection, or humiliation—we end up feeling anyway, and sometimes worse.

Our strength is in switching seats. Let God take control.

When you take your ego out of the equation, life is about Jesus and not about the self. This brings peace, humility, and a trust in God.

REFLECT:
What or whom are you trying to control?
Is it yours to control? (Remember that you can't control what others say, do, think, or feel.)
Is it for God alone?

YOU ARE INCOMPARABLE

I want you to say out loud, "I am incomparable."

I want you to say out loud, "There is no one like me."

I want you to remind yourself of those two sentences often. Why? Because you will experience moments of competition, tests, and mental challenges.

When your friends, peers, parents, pastors, teammates, teachers, siblings, and social media contacts try to prevent you from recognizing how unique and special you are, you can remind yourself that God made you unlike anyone else on this planet.

God doesn't want you to compare yourself to others by looking down and belittling them or looking left and right, thinking less of yourself. Rather, he wants you to look up and remember that God created you with a unique purpose in mind. Comparison breeds doubt, which will hinder your purpose and crush your self-worth until you lose touch with the very essence of your true self and how God created you.

REFLECT:

Do you compare yourself to others?
Change your perspective and focus on the unique gifts God gave you.

LIVE A LIFE OF PURITY

The acts of the flesh are obvious: sexual immorality, impurity and debauchery.
—Galatians 5:19

Let God be your GPS. If you follow the tracking system called the Bible and Holy Spirit, it will lead you to your destination and prevent you from getting lost on your journey of life. It is God's desire for you to live pure in all areas of your life.

Not having sex outside of marriage isn't the only form of purity. Having self-control over your body's desire to give in to sexual temptation is a form of purity. This means checking in with your thoughts, words, and actions. Touching women and speaking inappropriately is not holy and honorable in God's eyes. If you are making out with a woman who isn't your wife, you could possibly be touching another man's future wife. People who don't live for God won't see a problem with engaging in impure acts; however, it makes them a slave to lust.

Purity is a way of life to keep you safe from the enemy's traps. When we wait on God's timing and do it his way, the long-term benefits outweigh the short-term excitement.

REFLECT:
Choose an accountability partner (your dad, your youth pastor, someone you respect as a Christian) and check in with this person when you slip. You will inevitably have weak moments in your words, deeds, or thoughts, so make sure you are comfortable telling this person your failures as well as your successes.

YOU WON'T KNOW UNTIL YOU ASK

May he give you the desire of your heart and make all your plans succeed.
—Psalm 20:4

What makes you think that you can get a full-ride scholarship to a college?

Why do you believe that your parents will stay together?

How do you plan on getting a new car without the money to pay for it?

What makes you think that you will marry the woman of your dreams and not settle for less?

These were just a few of my prayers that people thought were outlandish, crazy, and unattainable. But at heart, my prayers were for education, for love, for capability, and for health. I was blessed to see my prayers answered. These were not selfish. These prayers were laced with bringing glory to God. My prayers for helping others through fitness as well as inspiring others to be successful were in line with God's will for my life. In this Scripture—"may he give you the desire of your heart"—King David had one prayer, and that was to protect God's people. He knew it was a good prayer because it was aligned with the will of God.

When our prayers are aligned with God's glory and are not selfish, we can operate with a stronger faith to see them come to pass. I'll be honest with you—you may not see every outlandish dream come true. That's okay. But how will you know if your prayer could be answered if you don't ask? You miss out on every prayer you don't pray. Align yourself with God's plan, and have the faith to pray outlandish prayers.

REFLECT:
Write an outlandish list. Pray before you do it; ask God to reveal the deepest desires of your heart, and don't hold back. Then watch God work.

REFERENCES

1. Page 29: National Center for Education Statistics. "Student Reports of Bullying: Results from the 2015 School Crime Supplement to the National Crime Victimization Survey." Institute of Education Sciences. December 2016. https://nces.ed.gov/pubs 2017/2017015.pdf

2. Page 48: Ritchie, Hannah and Max Roser. "Mental Health." OurWorldInData.org. April 2018. https://ourworldin data.org /mental-health

3. Page 50: Promises Treatment Centers. "How Many Teens Die of Drug Overdose?" https://www.promises.com/resources/overdose /many-teens-die-drug-overdose

4. Page 71: Patchin, Justin W. "2016 Cyberbullying Data." Cyberbullying Research Center. November 26, 2016. https://cyberbullying .org/2016-cyberbullying-data

5. Page 76: Centers for Disease Control and Prevention. "Health Effects of Secondhand Smoke." https://www.cdc.gov/tobacco/data _statistics/fact_sheets/secondhand_smoke/health_effects/index.htm

6. Page 118: Livingston, Gretchen. "Fewer Than Half of U.S. Kids Today Live in a 'Traditional' Family." Pew Research Center. December 22, 2014. http://www.pewresearch.org/fact-tank/2014/12/22 /less-than-half-of-u-s-kids-today-live-in-a-traditional-family

INDEX OF TOPICS

ABOUT THE AUTHOR

Andy Dooley is committed to empowering the next generation of leaders as a passionate Youth Director at Elevation Church in Charlotte, North Carolina. He has been working with young people for over 18 years, through sports, fitness, and ministry. Andy was named the 2016 Face of Reebok One, which allowed him to expand his platform of helping people understand and implement a holistic approach to spirituality and health. He is happily married to Tiffany, and they have three gorgeous children, Hope, Skylee, and Andy II.

You can visit his blog at AndyLDooley.com.

CPSIA information can be obtained
at www.ICGtesting.com
Printed in the USA
BVHW051229120620
581305BV00013B/245